THE UNAUTHORIZED HISTORY OF

THE UNAUTHORIZED HISTORY OF

ARE YOU READY?

TRIPLE H & SHAWN MICHAELS

WITH AARON WILLIAMS

WITH A SPECIAL FOREWORD BY

SHAWN MICHAELS & TRIPLE H

POCKET BOOKS

NEW YORK LONDON TORONTO SYDNEY

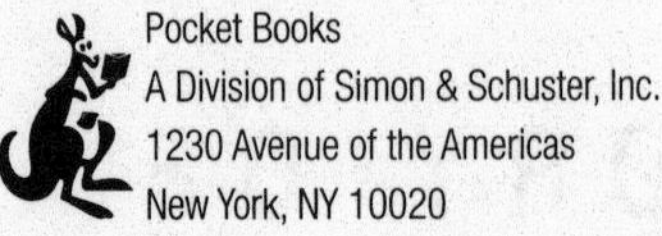

Pocket Books
A Division of Simon & Schuster, Inc.
1230 Avenue of the Americas
New York, NY 10020

This book is a publication of Pocket Books, a division of Simon & Schuster, Inc., under exclusive license from World Wrestling Entertainment, Inc.

First Pocket Books trade paperback edition October 2009

Designed by Ruth Lee-Mui

Manufactured in the United States of America

10 9 8 7 6 5 4 3 2 1

ISBN 978-1-4391-3727-7
ISBN 978-1-4391-6662-8 (ebook)

Are you ready?
You think you can tell us what to do?
You think you can tell us what to wear?
You think that you're better?
Well, you better get ready to bow to the masters
Break it down

D-Generate into something, fool
We just got tired of doing what you told us to do
And that's the breaks, boy
Yeah, that's the breaks, little man
Break it down
D-Generation X
D-Generation . . .
You think you can tell me what to do?
Do you know who you're talking to?

Better get used to the way the ball bounces
I see what you got and it measures in ounces
But that's the breaks, boy
Yeah, that's the damn breaks, little man
D-Generation X
D-Generation . . .
You think you're a big man?
I'll treat you like a little man . . .

Can you tell me what it's like to be half a man?
Must break your heart to see what I am
But that's the breaks, boy
Yeah, well, that's the breaks, little man . . .

Just stop wanting me to be someone else
Put it away like a book on the shelf that you can't read, boy,
Yeah, that you can't read . . .

FOREWORD

"For the thousands in attendance and the millions watching around the world, and for Vince McMahon, who we've basically driven crazy and may be in some nut farm as I speak . . ."

"Whoa, whoa, whoa, Hunter. This isn't a television show. This is a book. You can't start a book this way."

"Why not, Shawn? Isn't it you who said, 'DX does whatever it wants when it wants'?"

"Yeah, but . . . actually, good point, Hunter. I stand corrected. I guess that's why they call you Cerebral Assassin."

"Yes they do, Shawn, yes they do. Now if you'll excuse me, I'd like to get going here because I think the people reading this want to get on to the meat of this book."

"The meat?"

"Now . . . for the thousands reading this book, and the millions who aren't but hopefully will real soon—that means go tell all your friends about this book—let's get ready to . . ."

Dear Readers,

We, D-Generation X, Shawn Michaels and Triple H, would like to thank you for purchasing our book.

"Which is available at WWEShop.com, bookstores across the country, and at online retailers."

"Um, Shawn, I think they probably know that, considering they're reading this now and already have the book."

"Good point, Hunter. Let's continue on, shall we?"

As we were saying, we'd like to thank you for purchasing our book. When word got out that we were penning a history of DX, people began asking us, "Shawn, Hunter—Hunter, Shawn—why are you guys writing a book about DX?"

Well, we are DX after all, and we generally—no, let's take that back, we *always* do what we want when we want. So the obvious answer is that we felt like writing a book, so we did.

But as is the case with most things DX, there is usually more going on than what meets the eye, and there is another very important reason why we decided to put pen to paper and recount the sometimes strange but always fun history of D-Generation X.

You see, not too long ago we were on the road and we happened to have some free time. So we went to a local bookstore, which we sometimes do to help stimulate our brains, and started to peruse the shelves.

What we saw horrified us. Right there sitting on the shelves and staring us in the face were two of the greatest literary abortions ever published: *Controversy Creates Cash* and *Hollywood Hulk Hogan.* Besides feeling the urgent need to toss our cookies, we both looked at each other and shook our heads.

We couldn't believe the general public was being subjected to this kind of punishment. We thought about the poor kids who might come in to the bookstore looking for a book on wrestling and then be forced to read that kind of garbage.

Something needed to be done. You, our fans—heck, even our enemies—deserved better than that. So right then and right there we decided to write a book that might actually be fun to read.

Now, we have to be honest with you. This book might be titled *The Unauthorized History of D-Generation X,* but the corporate pinheads at WWE did have to be involved. So we couldn't give you all the dirt—this is a family-friendly business that Hunter would like to see succeed for obvious reasons, but we do promise to entertain you.

We hope you will enjoy this trip back in time, and if you don't, well, we got two words for you . . .

Sincerely,
Shawn and Hunter

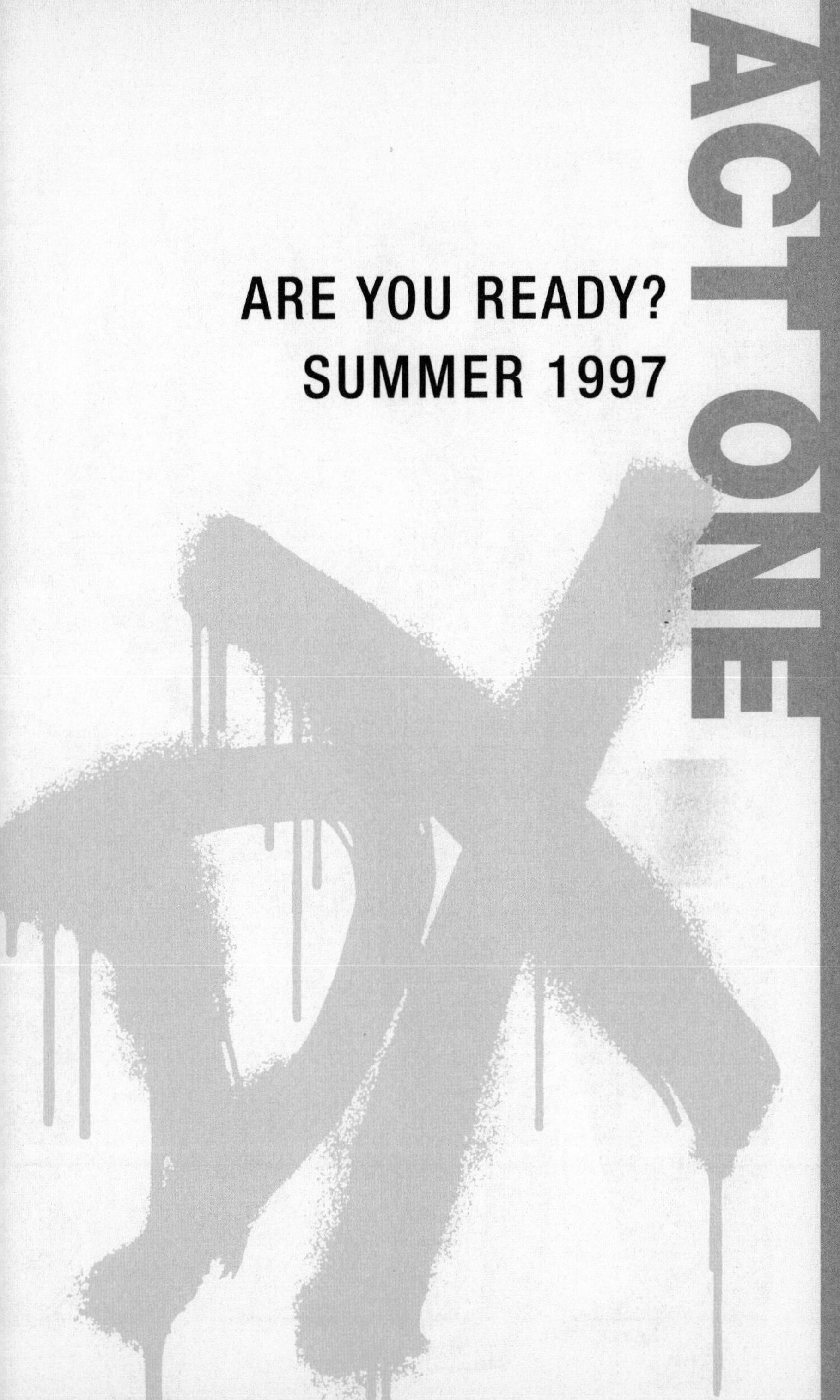

ACT ONE

ARE YOU READY?
SUMMER 1997

THE PLAYERS

D-GENERATION X

Shawn Michaels: a.k.a. Showstopper; the Icon; Main Event; Heartbreak Kid; HBK. The two-time World Wrestling Federation Champion and resident bad boy.

Triple H: a.k.a. Hunter Hearst-Helmsley; Hunter. Shawn Michaels's best friend. Known for his quick wit, ring psychology, and exceptionally large genitalia.

Chyna: a.k.a. the Ninth Wonder of the World; Joanie. Triple H's former bodyguard known for beating up male Superstars and increasing her breast size.

OTHER KEY PLAYERS

The Kliq: Wrestling buddies Shawn Michaels, Triple H, Kevin Nash (Diesel), Scott Hall (Razor Ramon), and Sean Waltman (X-Pac). Controversial group determined to change the nature of sports entertainment.

Rick Rude: a.k.a. the Ravishing One; "Ravishing" Rick Rude.

Former WWE Superstar known for disparaging out-of-shape sweathogs. Now employed as Shawn Michaels's enforcer.

Chief Jay Strongbow: a.k.a. Chief Jay. World Wrestling Federation Tag Team Champion in the 1970s and 80s. Currently working as an agent. He is a strong proponent of the old ways of doing business.

Undertaker: a.k.a. the Dead Man; the Prince of Darkness; the Phenom. Two-time World Wrestling Federation Champion feuding with Shawn Michaels. He and Michaels fight in what many regard as the greatest match in WWE history: the original Hell in a Cell at *Badd Blood*.

Sean Waltman: a.k.a. 1-2-3 Kid; X-Pac. Member of The Kliq, friend of Shawn and Triple H, generally credited for bringing the crotch chop to World Wrestling Federation.

Bret Hart: a.k.a. Hit Man. Shawn Michaels's archrival, who refuses to do business at *Survivor Series*, quits the company, and inadvertently helps catapult the company back to the top of the sports entertainment world.

Sgt. Slaughter: a.k.a. Sgt. Slobber; Sarge. Former World Wrestling Federation Champion and current commissioner. Sarge continuously tries to discipline D-Generation X. His overproductive salivary glands are a constant source of amusement for DX.

Vince McMahon: The owner of World Wrestling Federation, who also serves as a television announcer. He becomes a verbal target of DX, beginning one of the longest running feuds in sports entertainment history.

Jim Ross: a.k.a. J.R.; Good Ol' J.R. Beloved television announcer known for his passionate play-by-play calls. His disgust for DX is exemplified in such calls as: "This is like interviewing the ninth-grade gym class!" "Look at these jackasses!" and "They are repulsive!"

Davey Boy Smith: European Champion who gets screwed out of his title by DX in his hometown of Birmingham, England.

Ken Shamrock: a.k.a. World's Most Dangerous Man. Shawn and Hunter are concerned that this good friend of Bret Hart just might shoot on Shawn Michaels at the D-Generation X Pay-Per-View.

The Headbangers: An obnoxious tag team that has the gall to interrupt a game of DX strip poker.

Owen Hart: Entertaining Superstar and brother of Bret who battles with Triple H over the European Championship.

Arn Anderson: a.k.a. Double A. He has no role in the upcoming drama except for the fact that his nickname serves as the inspiration for Triple H's name.

Doink the Clown: A disturbed clown who doesn't do much for Shawn and Hunter.

Mankind: Rough and tough WWE Superstar who looks suspiciously like Cactus Jack and Dude Love.

Crush: Kona, Hawaii, native who gets the DX sense of humor.

Michael Cole: Television announcer who becomes the brunt of many DX jokes and ends up on the receiving end of a superatomic wedgie.

Mike Tyson: a.k.a. the Baddest Man on the Planet. Former heavyweight boxing champion who is involved in one of the great triple crosses in sports entertainment history.

Stone Cold Steve Austin: a.k.a. Stone Cold; the Rattlesnake. World's toughest S.O.B., who fights Shawn Michaels for the World Wrestling Federation Championship at *WrestleMania XIV*.

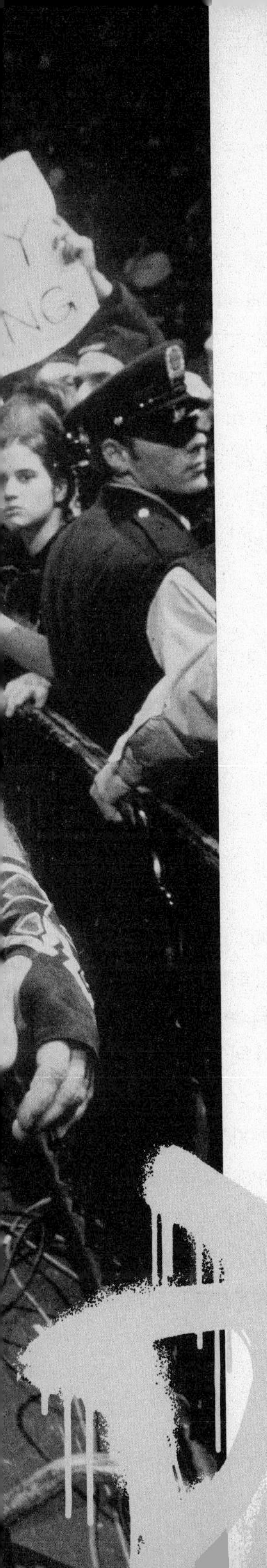

NEW GROUND

SHAWN MICHAELS

"Hey, that's May 19, 1996, at Madison Square Garden! That's Razor! That's Big Daddy Cool Diesel! Wait, that's you, Triple H. There I am. Hey wait! You were a bad guy! I was a good guy! What are we doing together?

"That was supposed to be Vince McMahon's biggest day. The first time Madison Square Garden had been sold out in some time . . . Oh Vin man, what's the matter? That subject still a little too sensitive for you, Vin Man? Vinnie Mac, what's-a matter? Is your dad rolling over in his grave? The family tradition in the McMahons, has it come to an end because me and my buddies made an ass out of you? C'mon, you were an ass long before I made one out of you!

"Now, I know what you are saying. 'Shawn, dammit, how many times have I told you.' "

VINCE MCMAHON

"I've had enough of this crap!"

TRIPLE H

"He might fire us! Look out! He might fire us!"

SHAWN: Our story begins a long, long time ago in the summer of 1997. It was so long ago that Hunter hadn't even won a European, much less an Intercontinental or World Championship. Friday night *SmackDown!*—still two years from its debut, which happened to be on a Thursday—wasn't even a figment of a figment in Vince McMahon's imagination. ECW was a regional promotion running bingo halls in the Northeast, and most of the current WWE roster had yet to embark upon their wrestling careers. John Cena was still in college, Randy Orton was in high school, and I'm not sure that guys like Cody Rhodes and Ted DiBiase, Jr., were even born yet.

HUNTER: Back then, Shawn was a very angry young man.

SHAWN: Wait a minute, Hunter, did you have to start with that so early in our story?

HUNTER: Well, it's true and part of the story, isn't it?

SHAWN: Yeah, but your first words in the whole story?

HUNTER: OK, how's this? At the time, World Wrestling Federation, as WWE was known back then, was locked in a bitter battle for survival with its archenemy, World Championship Wrestling.

SHAWN: Much better.

HUNTER: Continuing on . . . Thanks to former World Wrestling Federation stars like our good friends Kevin Nash and Scott Hall, WCW was drawing more television viewers and creating more buzz than World Wrestling Federation. We were in trouble. Many believed we would forever play second fiddle to WCW. Some thought we might even go out of business.

SHAWN: The mood inside our company reflected its real-world troubles. Both wrestlers and management were feeling the pressure. The atmosphere backstage at arenas was tense, and everyone was on edge.

HUNTER: The company's two biggest stars, Shawn and Bret Hart, basically hated each other, and their personal animosity was dividing the locker room in two—a lopsided two, with 90 percent on Bret's side and a handful on ours.

You see, back then Shawn was a very angry young man.

SHAWN: All right, go ahead. It's true.

HUNTER: Now professionally, Shawn was at the top of his game and firmly established as one of, if not *the,* best performer in the business. Personally, though, he was a bit of a mess. He was prone to bouts of anger and took every opportunity to alienate those who caused him the slightest inconvenience. To say that Shawn was not popular in the locker room would be a gross misunderstatement.
SHAWN: My good friend Triple H had problems of his own. Unfortunately, most were of my doing. While he was quiet and respectful to both management and fellow wrestlers, his loyalty to me gave those who disliked me the excuse to dislike him. So while Hunter may have had a few more friends in the locker room than me, he didn't have many. He also happened to be coming out of a year of "exile" within the company.

SHAWN: On May 19, 1996, Hunter, myself, Kevin Nash, and Scott Hall "broke kayfabe" by acknowledging our friendship and taking a bow—our Curtain Call—together in front of a sold-out Madison Square Garden audience. To many old-timers in management, this act was an affront to the profession. Heels and babyfaces were not supposed to be friends! If fans knew that wrestlers did not actually hate each other in real life, they would never come to matches! This was an old philosophy that no longer held true, but it was the philosophy that still held sway in World Wrestling Federation.

In order to assuage all the anger backstage, Vince McMahon had to do something. Otherwise he risked losing the trust of most of the people around him, men who had served him for a long time. Kevin and Scott were off to WCW so there was nothing Vince could do to them. I was one of the company's big stars, so punishing me would only end up hurting the company. So while Vince forced me to apologize to many in the back, he did not punish me.

Hunter, however, was a different story. He was just another mid-carder at this point in his career. He had all the talent in the world, but he was not established. He could be punished, and he was. Plans to have him win *King of the Ring* in June 1996 were quickly shelved, and for the next year he floundered in mid- and lower-card purgatory. He lost most of his matches and never got a real chance to move up the ladder.
HUNTER: The company's reaction to the Curtain Call really spoke volumes about

its approach to business. It was stuck in a bygone era that kept fans away from the back side of the business, treating fans as if characters were real and other wrestling organizations did not exist.

The world had changed. Many fans knew, at least to some degree, what was going on behind the scenses; and, just as important, they were desperate for more. The more they knew, the more they wanted to learn. For many fans, what was going on in the back was more interesting than the comparatively vanilla story lines that were playing out on TV. Still, World Wrestling Federation was stuck in its old ways. Most in management were either oblivious to or wary of the change, and they lobbied hard to continue with the old ways of doing business.

SHAWN: Despite the lobbying from those who wanted to stick with the old ways of doing business, we really believed that World Wrestling Federation had to change. We believed that we had the talent to rebound; and, if pushed in the right direction, we could once again regain sports entertainment supremacy.

HUNTER: We didn't sit down one day and say "Hey, let's revolutionize the business." We just wanted to help take the company in a new, different direction. The world had changed, but our product hadn't. We were still treating fans like they didn't know anything about the business. For instance, everyone knew we were in this huge battle with WCW, but on our show, WCW didn't even exist. Why didn't we talk about it on our show?

SHAWN: And it wasn't like we had this sudden revelation. We had been talking about moving in a new direction for a long time. Back in 1995, we had a meeting with Vince in Indianapolis, where Hunter, Kevin, and Scott talked about moving in a new direction, making our show more edgy and realistic. As a company, we had moved a little, but not enough to make that big a difference.

HUNTER: I remember after the Curtain Call, because I caught all the heat for it. Vince cut this promo on me, and I almost got fired. I was taking all the crap that went down. I had to go to all the agents and apologize. I went to them all, and all the old guys were cutting these promos on me about how we were disrespectful and how we were hurting the business.

I specifically remember Chief Jay Strongbow cutting this promo on me about breaking kayfabe. He's telling me that nobody knows that Shawn Michaels,

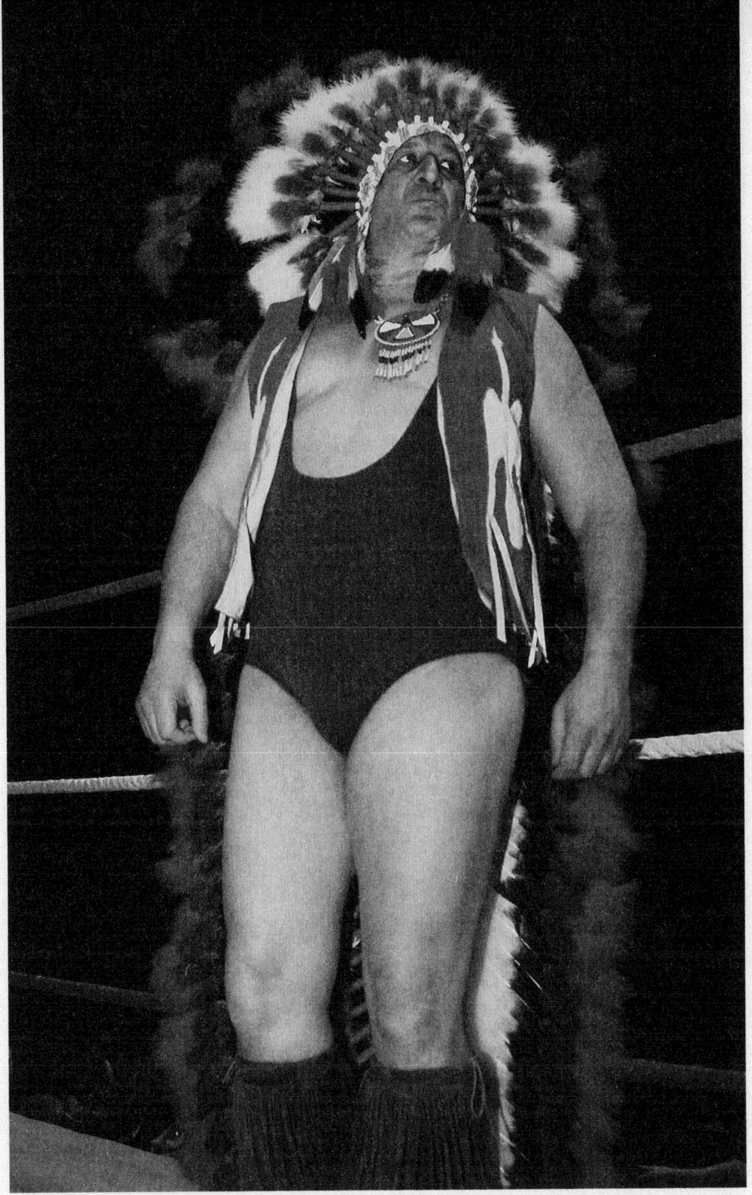

The Curtain Call brought a single tear to the eye of Chief Jay Strongbow.

Scott Hall, and Hunter Hearst-Helmsley are friends. They—the fans—don't know, and we shouldn't let them into that side of the business.

As he's cutting this promo on me, I'm sitting there thinking if nobody knows about it, why are 18,000 people in Madison Square Garden going nuts? Why?

Because they all knew the back side of the business. And because the back side of the business had been hidden for so long, it was almost more interesting than the front side. It was definitely more interesting back then.

The fact that Shawn and Bret couldn't stand each other and were having this verbal warfare of words on TV about things in their personal lives was way more interesting than watching Doink the Clown come out and do whatever he did.

SHAWN: The other thing is that we had also been discussing that we wanted to have fun. At this point in my career, I really wasn't having much fun. And Hunter really is a funny guy. The way Hunter carried himself around back then was very different. When he was riding around in the car with us, he was one of the funniest guys around. But he was never like that around other guys in the business. When he was around them, he always handled himself in a straight manner.

During the summer of 1997, he and I and Chyna were on the *Wrestle Vessel*, a cruise where fans could come and meet WWE Superstars. We were sitting around at dinner one night and started talking about working together and doing a tag team. We talked about how Hunter could bring out his funny side. The characters he had been playing to that point wouldn't allow him to do that. I felt strongly that it was time to bring that funny side out.

HUNTER: There is this stuffy, serious side to the business, and yet there is such an opportunity to have fun with it. Ninety percent of the time, it seemed like it was no fun. Everything was so serious. Now, I'm a proponent of the serious side of the business, but if all you ever watched were dramas, and that was it, there's no letup. It gets tiring and boring. We wanted to make wrestling fun again.

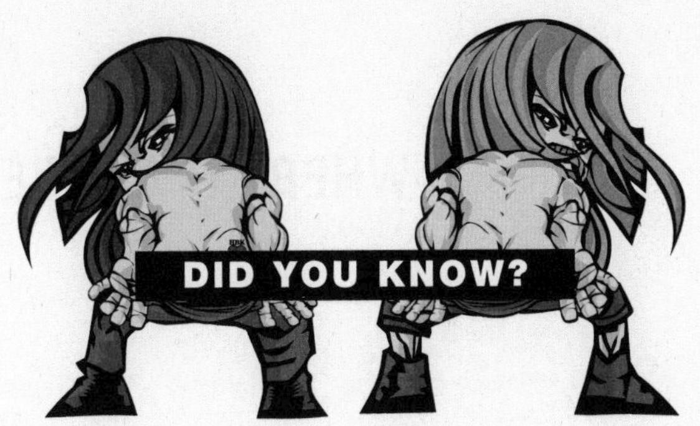

It was Shawn Michaels who came up with the name Triple H.

SHAWN: Yep, I'll take credit for that. Not too long after the meeting in Indianapolis, The Kliq was sitting around talking. Everyone at the time had some sort of gimmick, so I asked Hunter, "What do you want to be called? Paul? Hunter?"

Hunter replied that he wasn't sure, so I suggested Triple H.

I stole the idea from Double A, Arn Anderson. So it wasn't the most original idea, but it worked out pretty darn well.

WHERE IT ALL BEGAN

HUNTER: We had wanted to work with each other for a long time. Both of our strengths are making other people look good, and we knew it would work; and we knew we could have a lot of fun doing it. It was just something that always kept coming up all the time in conversation. We would ask to be put together and always be told no for one reason or another.

SHAWN: We finally got the opportunity to work together right after *SummerSlam*. I was going to turn heel and start working a program with Undertaker. I had never worked with 'Taker before because Vince didn't think that people would buy someone of my size being able to beat him. But Vince thought with Hunter and Chyna at my side, along with Rick Rude, who was going to be my "insurance policy," me beating Undertaker was way more than plausible.

Our first actual match together was against Undertaker & Mankind in Atlantic City. We nailed 'Taker a couple of times with a chair and the place just exploded with hate toward us.

HUNTER: You have to understand, weapons weren't used that often back then, and *no one* got to Undertaker. Shawn hit him with the chair, and then he did the sit-up and we ran like the cowards we were. I just remember all the heat we got that night and me thinking: *This could be huge.*

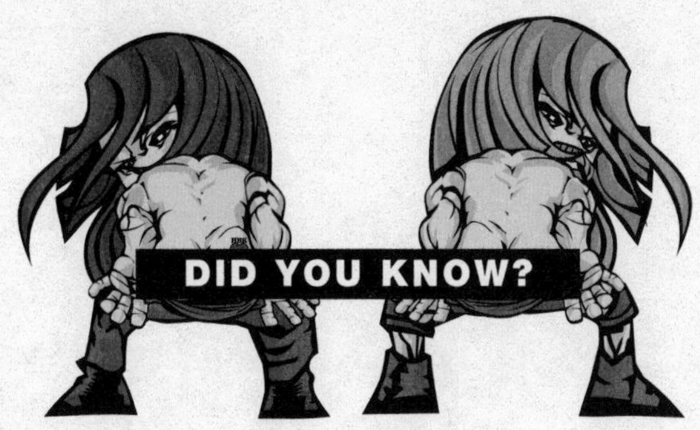

Shawn and Hunter first met at *WrestleMania XI*.

SHAWN: Kevin Nash and I were sitting backstage when an unfamiliar face walked up to us and said, "I don't want to interfere with what you guys are doing, but my name is Paul Levesque. I talked to Terry Taylor [when I was in WCW] and he said you are the guys to hang out with. So if you don't mind, I'd like to hang out and travel with you."

HUNTER: I'd been in the company for a little bit and rode with a few other guys. It was one of those things where you ride with someone for ten minutes, and you're like, "I can't wait to get out of here." With these guys, The Kliq, I jumped in the car, and even though the first night Kid got a little out of control, and part of me was thinking, "What am I doing with these guys," I really felt like I fit. Five minutes into the ride and it just feels comfortable. We were all on the same wavelength.

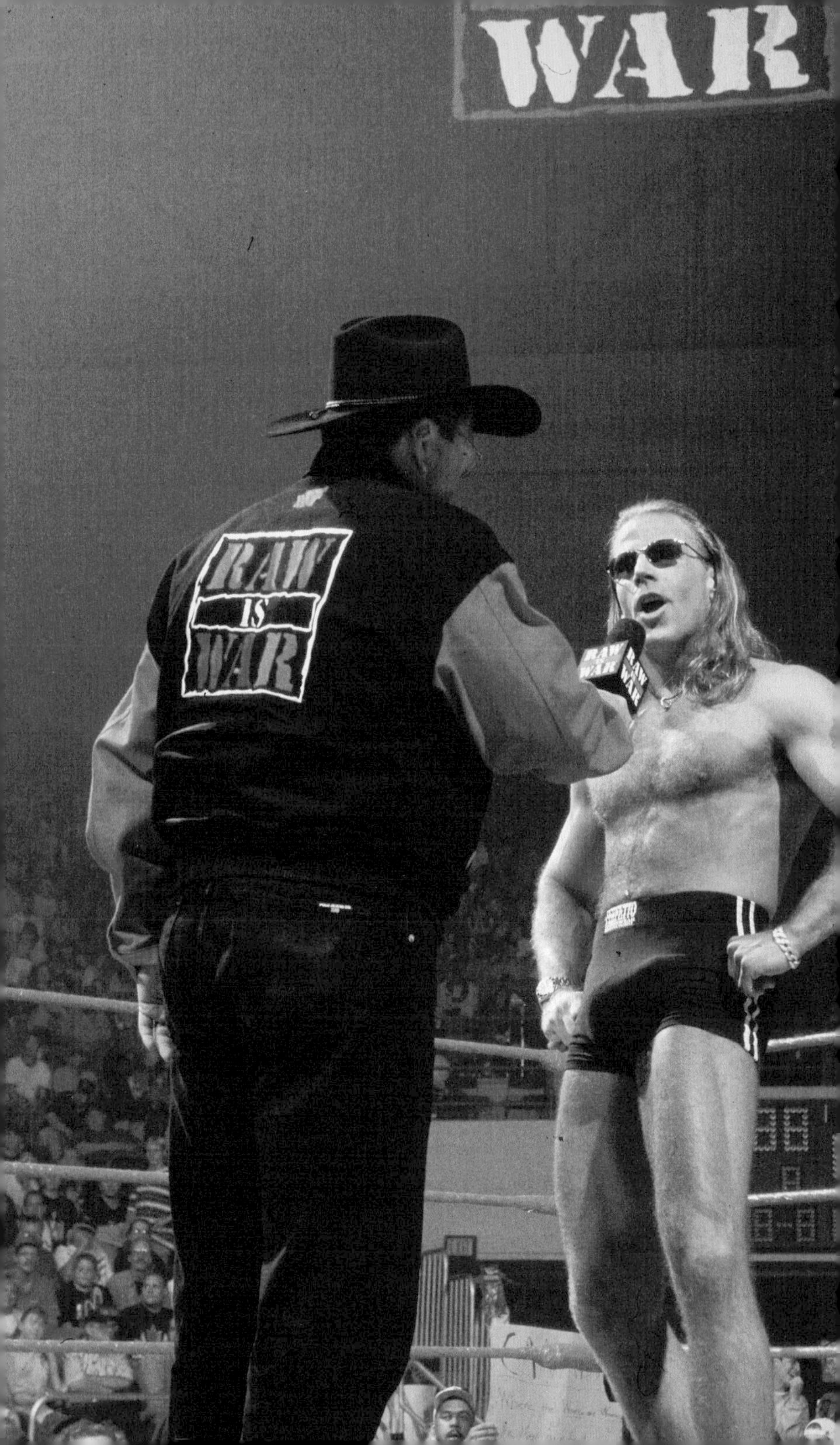
WAR
RAW IS WAR
RAW IS WAR

KICKING IT UP

HUNTER: One month after we had made our tag team debut in Atlantic City, and one week after Chyna and I had interfered on behalf of Shawn during his match with Undertaker at the *Ground Zero* Pay-Per-View, Shawn was set to do an interview with Jim Ross. The purpose of the interview was to build interest for Shawn and Undertaker's upcoming Hell in a Cell match at *Badd Blood*. Shawn was supposed to call out Undertaker, and 'Taker, who was not at the show, would come up on the Titantron and threaten Shawn, who would act all scared. The plan was nothing out of the ordinary, but with the two of us, the ordinary wasn't going to be ordinary any longer . . .

SHAWN: Before the interview, I was walking around the back in these skintight biker shorts that I used to wear just because I knew it annoyed a lot of people. As a joke, I stuffed a roll of gauze down my pants and started goofing around. Right before I was set to go out and do my interview with

J.R., Brian Adams—Crush—double dog dared me to go out in the arena and on television with the gauze in my shorts.

I was never one to turn down a double dog dare, so I gathered everyone at a television monitor and went out there fully loaded with my gauze. J.R. was trying to do a serious interview, but I was jumping around, bumping and grinding, the gauze was pretty evident, and I cut the most over-the-top promo. I was having a blast and I knew all the boys in the back were loving it. I finally called Undertaker out and he came up on the screen and threatened me. That part worked fine. J.R., though, was understandably angry over my making a mockery of his interview. He left the ring to go back to his announcing position, and I decided to have a little fun.

I grabbed the mic, knowing full well that Undertaker wasn't there, and yelled, "You know what, if Undertaker is so tough, why doesn't he come out and fight me right now?"

The crowd exploded, hoping to see us go at it right there.

"Undertaker," I continued, "let's do it right here, right now. If you don't come out here by the count of ten, that means you are afraid of me." I counted to ten. "See, he's afraid of me!" I came to the back and the boys thought it was the funniest thing they had ever heard.

The next day, Vince called me. "I'm fining you $10,000 for that incident last night."

"What for?"

"You humiliated the company and Undertaker." He went on this long tirade about how I was unprofessional and rude to J.R.

"I have to tell you something: I thought it was funny. Everyone thought it was funny. Ross was hot? That's funny stuff. Don't you think it's funny? People do that all the time. I wasn't the first guy to stick gauze down my pants."

"Well, you offended some women in the [production] truck."

"Are you sure?"

"Yes."

"I don't think that's true." Hunter had been on the headset while I was out there, and he told me that some women were laughing about it. "That's not what I heard, Vince. I heard they thought it was pretty funny too."

"That's not the point."

"That *is* the point. It is funny. We are getting our backsides kicked in the ratings. We have to start doing better stuff. Our girls get boob jobs all the time. One week they come out they are flat and the next week they have huge breasts and nobody notices. The fans all see it. How come no one comments, 'Sable, did you get the mumps last week?' Gauze in the shorts, that's funny. You can't tell me that's not funny."

"It's just unprofessional and has nothing to do with our business."

"We need to start kicking it up."

HUNTER: Shawn called me up after he had spoken with Vince and told me he had been fined ten grand. I'm just glad they didn't fine me because I didn't have that back then. The thing is, it was a dare in the back. It was just goofing. This was the kind of stuff people did, or at least wanted to do. It's a bit juvenile, sure, but it's funny. Everyone in the back loved it, and it certainly got a reaction from the crowd.

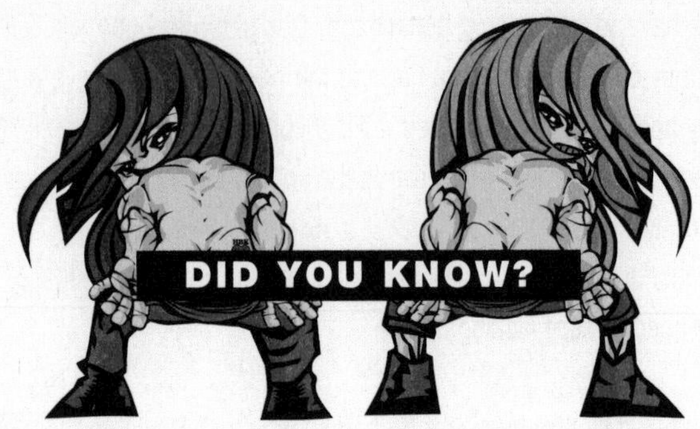

It was Sean Waltman, X-Pac, who brought the crotch chop to World Wrestling Federation.

SHAWN: Kid saw someone do it on a European tour in 1996, the one before Kevin, Scott, and Kid left for WCW. Kid started doing it, and then, when he left, we started doing it.

HUNTER: That was something we were doing in house shows and in the car long before it went on TV. Someone would throw a zinger at us, and we just fired back with the chop.

SHAWN: After we started using it, we started getting some heat because they thought it wasn't appropriate for television. They asked us to turn it into more of an X than a crotch chop. Then we turned it into a crotch thing with the X.

HUNTER: Of course, we did whatever would get the most heat and got admonished for doing the wrong type of chop quite a few times.

DX

OUR FIRST RIOT

SHAWN MICHAELS

"I want you to take a look at your champion [the British Bulldog] and then take a look at the new Grand Slam winner. Hart family, this is for you. And Diana Smith, sweetheart, this one is especially for you!"

TRIPLE H

"Take a look, Hart family, c'mon. This one's for you!"

VINCE MCMAHON

"What a dastardly human being! Michaels might be a great athlete, but look at him taunt this capacity crowd!"

SHAWN: Before we could get to my rematch with Undertaker at *Badd Blood* in October, we had to get through a special Pay-Per-View that was being held in Birmingham, England. Davey Boy Smith was the European Champion and he was from Birmingham. I told the creative team, "If you want to get me some heat, have me screw him for the title in his hometown." They loved the idea. Davey Boy was so over in England and he never lost there. Screwing him out of the title in front of his hometown fans was a good business decision because it would generate a ton of heat.

I had Hunter, Chyna, and Rick Rude assist me in applying a figure-four hold on Davey Boy and the referee stopped the bout. Then we started beating up on Davey Boy and going after his family, who were sitting ringside for the match. The crowd just went nuts. They were throwing beer, food, just about anything they could get their hands on at us. It was honest real heat in Birmingham. You know the European title didn't really mean a darn thing, and I mean everyone in that place wanted to kill us.

HUNTER: I just wanted to confirm that it really was that close to a full-blown riot—people were throwing bottles at us. When we got out of there, when we were backing up the ramp, I remember thinking any second these people are going to come after us. It was very intense.

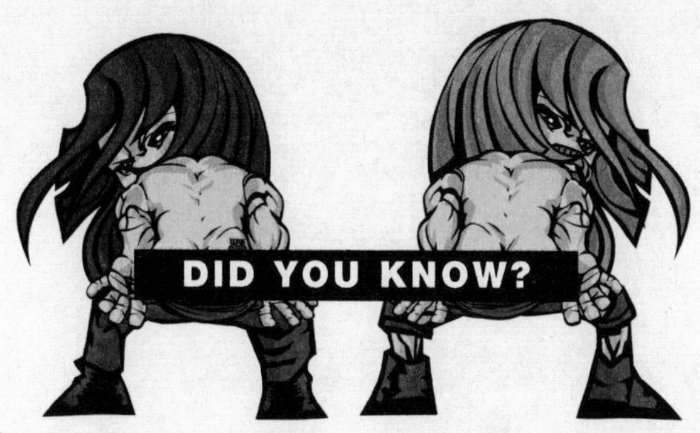

Shawn was once fired from WWE.

SHAWN: It was back in January 1987. After my first match, me and my tag team partner, Marty Jannetty, went out to socialize with other Superstars and ended up getting into an altercation with Jimmy Jack Funk. By the time word got back to Vince McMahon about what had happened, a little brouhaha had turned into a full-blown riot. We pleaded our case to Vince, but he felt that the other Superstars just didn't want us around. In order to preserve some harmony in the locker room, Vince decided to let us go. A year and a half later, we got a call inviting us back to rejoin the company.

HUNTER: I guess I'm one of the only Superstars who's never heard Vince tell him, "You're fired!"

SHAWN: And for some reason, despite all you have been through with him, you seem to have this very close bond. I just don't see that ever happening.

I AM THE TEXPERT
I AM MAXMINI
RAW IS WAR
NBA

THE UNTHINKABLE

SHAWN MICHAELS

"Now Triple H, this is your chance, my friend. I want you to unload on the World Wrestling Federation because this is what you have been waiting for, buddy. Hit 'em!"

TRIPLE H

"The World Wrestling Federation and Vince McMahon. You've always been afraid of Kliqs, haven't you? Well, this is one Kliq that you are never going to break up: Hunter Hearst-Helmsley, Chyna, HBK!

"Now I've been sitting back for a couple of years while you and World Wrestling Federation have spread your legs like some cheap whore for all the so-called Superstars of World Wrestling Federation . . . when you know as well as I do that none of them, not one of them, could lace my boots. And my good friend just pointed that out to me. So now instead of sitting back and

letting you try and run things and waiting for my break, I am now taking it in my hands, and there is no stopping us now!"

SHAWN: In a little over a month, we had made ourselves into the most hated characters in the company. We had done it for the most part by acting like heels in the ring. We hadn't done that much yet in terms of incorporating backstage stuff into our onscreen behavior. In Albany, New York, on the September 29 edition of *Raw,* we ratcheted it up to a whole new level. In the middle of an interview that was supposed to build interest in my upcoming Hell in a Cell match with Undertaker but had veered so far off course that J.R. commented, "This is like interviewing the ninth-grade gym class," I encouraged Triple H to take the microphone from me and let loose on Vince. What happened next was unprecedented. Triple H started going after Vince McMahon, not for things that had been made up for television, but for stuff that had happened in real life.

HUNTER: The first time I had to go out and cut a promo on Vince, I was scared to say the things that I really wanted to say. Vince came to me, and I asked, "How far do you want me to go with this?"

He said, "Say whatever you want to say."

So we go out there and the interview is going on and I get the microphone and just start going off on him. I remember when I said, "While you and World Wrestling Federation have spread your legs like some cheap whore for all the so-called Superstars of World Wrestling Federation . . . when you know as well as I do that none of them, not one of them, could lace my boots." I was referring to how I had been buried for the past year from the Curtain Call while other guys were moving forward with their careers. And I could just see his eyes change and him thinking, "You mother ****er."

Nobody talked to him like that, and I was saying that on live TV! I remember being scared to death to say it, but it really did feel good to get that out. And he wasn't hot about it. Well, he said he wasn't hot about it, but I could tell he was. And he wasn't the only one. Not many people in the locker room were happy with what we were doing.

SHAWN: What we were doing was pulling the veil back on people's characters. At that time Vince was just an announcer on TV. He wasn't playing the role of

Mr. McMahon yet. We started to say some of the taboo things that you weren't supposed to say. It was a little bit of a cross between being innovative and exposing, not really the business, but who people really were, and at the same time ourselves. It was a big risk. Most current and former wrestlers were opposed to showing the backstage part of the business to the fans. If we didn't get the immediate reaction we got, our careers were probably at stake.

I think that one of the big keys to us doing it, and doing it well, was us being who we were in the car traveling around. What we and everyone did was ride around and talk about the other guys and the business. That's what we started doing on TV.

HUNTER: We just took what we were doing for real after the shows and put it on TV.

We knew all that stuff that we said and the things we were going to say were controversial. But it was all stuff that we were really saying outside the ring. And that was the key. It was believable because it was real.

SHAWN: They quickly learned to be on the delay button all the time when we went out. We always said, "What's the worst thing they can do to us, fire us?"

HUNTER: We went under the premise that it's much better to beg for forgiveness than to ask for permission. We could always say, "We're sorry we crossed the line."

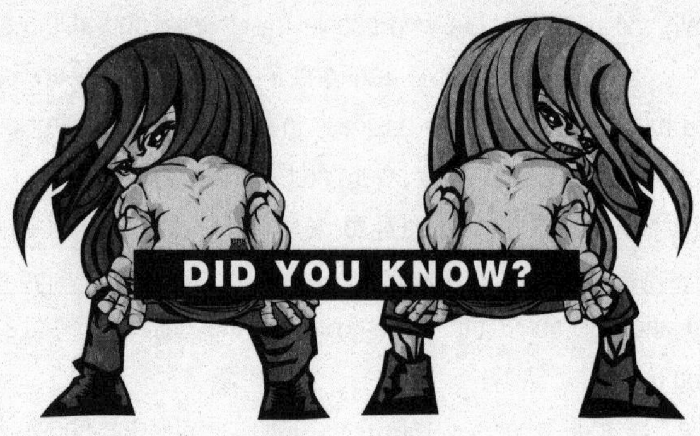

SHAWN: Vince started announcing wrestling matches way back in 1971, when he became the play-by-play announcer for his father's World Wide Wrestling Federation.

HUNTER: You said, "way back," not "stand back," right?

SHAWN: No, I said, "way back." Why, you feel like dancing?

HUNTER: No, Shawn, we'll get to that later. By the way, when you get a chance, check out the suits he wore back then. Really stylish.

SHAWN: Vince continued in this role until D-Generation X, Hunter and myself, exposed him as the owner of WWE in 1997. His twenty-six-year stint as the voice of WWE makes him the most tenured announcer in WWE history. Hall of Famer Jim Ross is second, with sixteen years under his belt.

BADD BLOOD

HUNTER: *Badd Blood* is best known for Shawn and Undertaker's epic Hell in a Cell battle. It was the first of its kind and generally regarded as one of the greatest matches in WWE history.

SHAWN: Thank you for those kind words, Hunter.

HUNTER: You're welcome. I'm sure you'll be mentioning some of my best matches later in this book.

SHAWN: I'm sure I will.

HUNTER: At this point the company was on a roll. Crowds were increasing and television ratings had started to rise. But while the numbers were improving, inside the locker room things were getting worse. We were more isolated than ever. We had exposed Vince and we were coming out with signs that said "Who booked this crap?" This kind of stuff really upset the so-called traditionalists, and the animosity between Shawn and Bret was growing. In short, the locker room was not a pleasant place to be.

Guys are telling us that what we are doing is horrible for business, which first of all flies in the face of reality. Then Shawn goes out and has a match like he did with Undertaker in the Hell in a Cell. We were delivering on all levels. I remember helping Shawn back through the Gorilla position and everybody looking at him. We had a lot of heat at that point. And he just yelled, "Follow that, ****ers." Now, he was very angry at the time, but the point is you can talk crap about what we were doing, but nobody else could go out and have a match like that. We were delivering, so get off us.

SHAWN: Looking back, I wish I had worded that differently. But for me, I just believed so much in what we were doing. What we were doing was good for the company.

I was feeling all the heat, and some was my fault and some was not. But I did feel bad for Hunter, because it was unfair to him. He was getting some heat for what we were doing, but he also was getting a lot just for being my friend.

In retrospect, I could take that attitude because I was an established star. Hunter was probably in a riskier position because he was just hitting his stride.

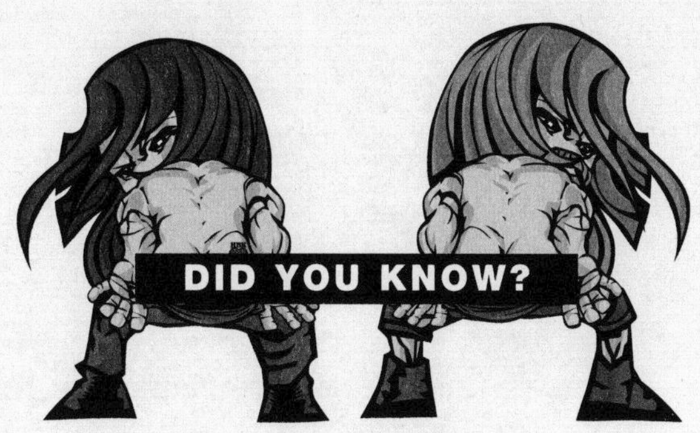

Most of the time Hunter and Shawn don't know what the other one is going to say before going out in front of the crowd and camera.

HUNTER: We don't script things out ahead of time. It's improv, reaction, and build as we go. It wouldn't work if we tried to script things out. We are mostly just entertaining ourselves. People like to see that we are enjoying ourselves, and if we are having fun, it helps lighten the mood even more and makes it more enjoyable for the fans because we are having fun with them. It's infectious. It's also original and more special when it's not scripted, and audiences like that. People feel it's not just a routine and that they are getting something original. Shawn and I know each other so well it's almost like we know where the other one is going without having to say it.

RAW
IS
WAR

THE CHRISTENING

HUNTER: On the night following *Badd Blood,* Michael Cole attempted to interview us.

SHAWN: Big mistake!

HUNTER: Huge mistake! Even bigger mistake wearing that Kevlar-like underwear that doesn't tear away.

SHAWN: It hurts just thinking about it. He didn't have to go to the hospital, did he?

HUNTER: He couldn't walk for a week and needed a case of Preparation H, but I don't think there was any permanent damage.

Let me explain. You see, before Cole could get started, we proffered up an appropriate World Wrestling Federation hello from The Kliq—a superatomic wedgie. I think for the next couple months he ran from us every time he saw us. Anyhow, after he limped out of the ring, Shawn took the microphone in his hands.

SHAWN: I started bragging about my win over Undertaker and told everyone I was going to show some footage from the match. When I asked the nimrods in back to play some footage from *Badd Blood*, nothing happened. Then video was shown from the Curtain Call incident back in 1996. The "switch" of footage allowed us to begin berating Vince McMahon and proclaim The Kliq as the most powerful force in the business.

HUNTER: In the middle of our promo, Bret Hart, Jim Neidhart, Owen Hart, and Davey Boy Smith came out to verbally confront us. Bret took to the microphone amid chants of "USA! USA!" and began by speaking to the audience that was booing the heck out of him.

BRET HART

"Boy Toy . . . yeah, you can go ahead and look at your big hero because this is what it's come down to. You have no self-respect for yourselves because you're looking at somebody that's got no respect for anything or anybody.

"Now Shawn Michaels, as for you, you are a disgrace to professional wrestling. You know I am a second-generation wrestler. I paid my dues like a lot of second-generation wrestlers, and you are nothing but the lowest form of scum that I have ever come across.

"Shawn Michaels, you are nothing but a degenerate. And I think I know as well as the rest of The Hart Foundation knows what the H in HHH stands for and the H in HBK stands for. You are nothing but a homo, and the guy in the green shirt [Hunter] is nothing but a homo . . . and the fact is I make more money than all three of you guys combined in the ring . . . You know, Shawn Michaels, The Kliq—your two boyfriends, Diesel and Razor—I ran those two guys out of town, and I'm going to run both of you out of town. And you know what? I'm going to start with that degenerate right beside you in the green shirt, Hunter Hearst-Helmsley. Tonight I issue you a challenge to step in the ring with the best there is, the best there was, and the best there ever will be."

SHAWN: I think I had a very mature, well-thought-out response to his verbal assault. I believe it went something like, "*Ooooooooooooooh!! I've got two words for 'Hit Man' Bret Hart: Suck it!*"

So the match was set that night for Hunter and Bret, and Hunter beat

Oh Canada loved us . . . as much as they did in England.

Bret via countout after I superkicked him while Chyna distracted him. During the match I started picking my nose with Bret's Canadian flag. I didn't mean to offend any Canadians. I just figured it would get us some extra heat, which it certainly did.

HUNTER: The following week, *Raw* began with Vince interviewing Bret Hart. Bret was disparaging Shawn when Shawn, myself, Chyna, and Rick Rude appeared on the Titantron. They showed the footage of Shawn sticking the Canadian flag up his nose and my victory over Bret. In response, Bret called us degenerates again. This time, we didn't disagree.

SHAWN MICHAELS

"And you talk about us being degenerates? You know, I'm tired of Generation X getting a bad rap. Are you a degenerate? I'm positive I am one."

TRIPLE H

"I guess I have to be one."

SHAWN MICHAELS

"Generation X always gets a bad rap, everyone calling us degenerates. D-Generation X, is that us? D-Generation X. Triple H, HBK, Chyna—we are D-Generation X. You make the rules and we will break them!"

Generation X consists of those born between 1965 and 1976. There are currently 52 million Generation Xers in the United States. Not all of them are degenerates.

RAW
WAR

SGT. SLOBBER

SGT. SLAUGHTER

"I demand you to start showing me some respect!"

SHAWN MICHAELS

"OK, Sarge, we'll start showing you some respect. Suck it!"

TRIPLE H

"Sarge, you can call me maggot, you can spit all over the place . . . Do you know who we are? We are D-Generation X and this is World Wrestling Federation and we make the rules, not you. Get it?"

JIM ROSS

"The audacity of D-Generation X! They respect no one! How heinous can they be?"

SHAWN: Ever since Hunter and I started working together, Commissioner Sgt. Slaughter had done his best to try and discipline us. He constantly berated us about being disrespectful and often put us in matches he believed would serve as punishment. DX, of course, was not going to take Sarge's actions lying down. In one of our favorite moments, I called out Slaughter to make a match for me with Ken Shamrock for the week after *Survivor Series.*

HUNTER: Every week Sgt. Slaughter was coming out and cutting promos on us. The thing is, when he spoke, he really would spit and we would be covered in it.

SHAWN: Scientifically speaking, I believe he had a case of overactive salivary glands. I remember coming back after one of his spitting incidents and saying, "We have to do something with this."

HUNTER: But remember, it was said within that vein: "That was funny, imagine if we came out with face masks with wipers." We really didn't have a long-term game plan. It was a day-to-day thing. Stuff would come up from all sorts of places and we would just run with it.

SHAWN: You never knew where ideas would come from. Someone would say something that you just thought was stupid, but it brought something to mind and we just let it go.

HUNTER: We knew the destination we wanted to get to. We just had no idea what street we had to take to get there.

SHAWN: Sometimes that led to a little stress backstage with our production people. If *we* didn't know what we were going to do, they were *completely* in the dark.

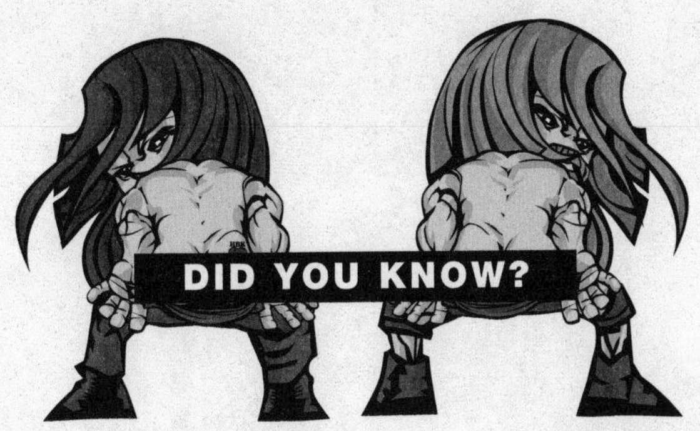

Sgt. Slaughter once put out a musical album titled *Sgt. Slaughter and Camouflage Rocks America*. It was 1985, and the two-time WWE Champion and future Hall of Famer was among the most popular athletes in all of sports. He took his shot at musical stardom by belting out such tunes as "The Cobra Clutch," "Love Your Country," The Hurt Is Gone," and a cover of Neil Diamond's "America."

THE NINTH WONDER OF THE WORLD

HUNTER: We first went to management with the idea of bringing Chyna in when they were looking for a bodyguard or manager for me in late '96 or very early '97. We had given them the idea of Shawn and I doing something together but they didn't want to do it. Then we gave them the idea about Chyna shortly after we met her. Vince thought it was stupid. "Who's going to believe that a girl is going to beat up a guy?" he said. "What, the guy's not tough enough so the girl is going to do it for him? They will hate that."

SHAWN: Fortunately, Shane was able to help convince Vince to bring Chyna in. We were talking with Shane about her in an IHOP in Tampa, and he loved the idea of a butt-kicking female bodyguard.

HUNTER: The night Vince said yes to Chyna was the same night Shawn gave up the Championship because of his knee injury and told everyone about his knee injury and gave his "I lost my smile" speech [February 13, 1997]. Vince came to me and said, "Shawn's hurt, he's going to take some time off. I'll bring that broad on, but she's your responsibility. If she screws up, it's your fault!"

SHAWN: Chyna had a couple of different roles with us. Outside of performing, she kept us focused and functioning. We'd come back from the ring and she'd have a protein shake for us. On traveling days, she'd get us up and take us to the gym.

HUNTER: As out there and as frazzled as we were, she kept us at least a little bit on track and moving ahead. She didn't know anything about the business. She didn't know a lot of the stuff we were talking about and doing. It was behind the scenes where she kept us moving ahead.

SHAWN: You could say that she fulfilled a little bit of a mothering aspect. I mean, Hunter did too for me at that point considering that I was pretty out there at the time.

HUNTER: But it's different when a woman is doing it. I mean, if I do too much of the mothering, we're borderline gay.

SHAWN: As far as performing went, she was great because she was so different. There was no skepticism on our part in having Joanie.

HUNTER: We knew how to make her work and how to protect her. She wouldn't move. She never flinched when guys got in her face. When she was going to pick up that two-hundred-eighty-pound guy she'd beat the crap out of him and then go back and stay still. We got in the ring with her and taught her how to work like a guy.

She really was just so fresh. Everything we were doing had never been done before, promo wise and ring wise. Her character was perfect because she was never in on the joke, even though she could be part of the joke. For instance, when she got her implants and it was blatantly obvious, the Old School way of doing things would have been to ignore it. We, of course, were all over it. Shawn was all over that, leaning on them, staring at them. The great thing about that was that she played it straight. She gave us someone to play off. Like when we were doing all the male genitalia jokes. It made us seem even more juvenile because there was a straight woman in there with us.

SHAWN: Another thing is that you never really knew where Joanie stood. Fans had to kind of wonder how she felt hanging out with those two juvenile goofs. And this was at a time when no one was doing subtle stuff. If you could pull that off, it was huge, and she was able to do just that. I think she contributed to a lot of our success.

HUNTER: In the ring, she also made us better heels. Everything we did played to that, that it takes two of us or more to get you down. Sometimes we'd be getting beat up, and Chyna would come in and stop our opponents. Then we'd beat them up. It was like the broad was making the save. We needed a woman to do our dirty work, and it made us that much more despised.

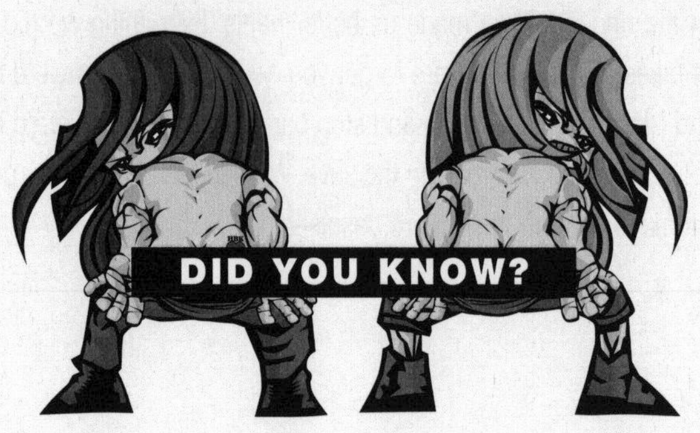

Shawn and Hunter met Chyna in Springfield, Massachusetts, the very same city in which the only D-Generation X Pay-Per-View was held. Coincidence? We think not.

DX

THE AFTERMATH

SHAWN MICHAELS

"Since *Survivor Series,* Shawn Michaels hasn't had a lot of sleep. There's a lot of controversy surrounding what happened at *Survivor Series*. I never thought that it would end that way. Bret Hart and Shawn Michaels have had their differences both personally and professionally. But never in my wildest dreams did I think it would come down to this. Bret, I want the world to know that I take full and total responsibility for what happened at *Survivor Series*. The world should know that Bret Hart is still under contract until November 30. Bret Hart deserved better. Vince McMahon and the [company] deserved better.

"I want everybody to know Bret Hart and Shawn Michaels have finally had contact with each other, without the knowledge of the media, without the knowledge of Vince McMahon, without the knowledge of the Internet, without the knowledge of the underground dirtsheet writers. I contacted Bret and he spoke to me, and Bret and I have an arrangement, an agreement.

"Bret Hart and Shawn Michaels tonight will settle this once and for all. And Bret, this is up to you. It can either end with a handshake, or it can end in a fight. The fact of the matter is, Bret Hart and Shawn Michaels will be here tonight in the ring, face to face, and this controversy will be done once and for all.

"Ladies and gentlemen, you've heard the rumor, it's time to put it all aside. Tonight the controversy comes to an end. Ladies and gentlemen, Bret 'Hit Man' Hart . . ."

TRIPLE H

"We always knew Bret was short on talent and short on charisma, but this is ridiculous!"

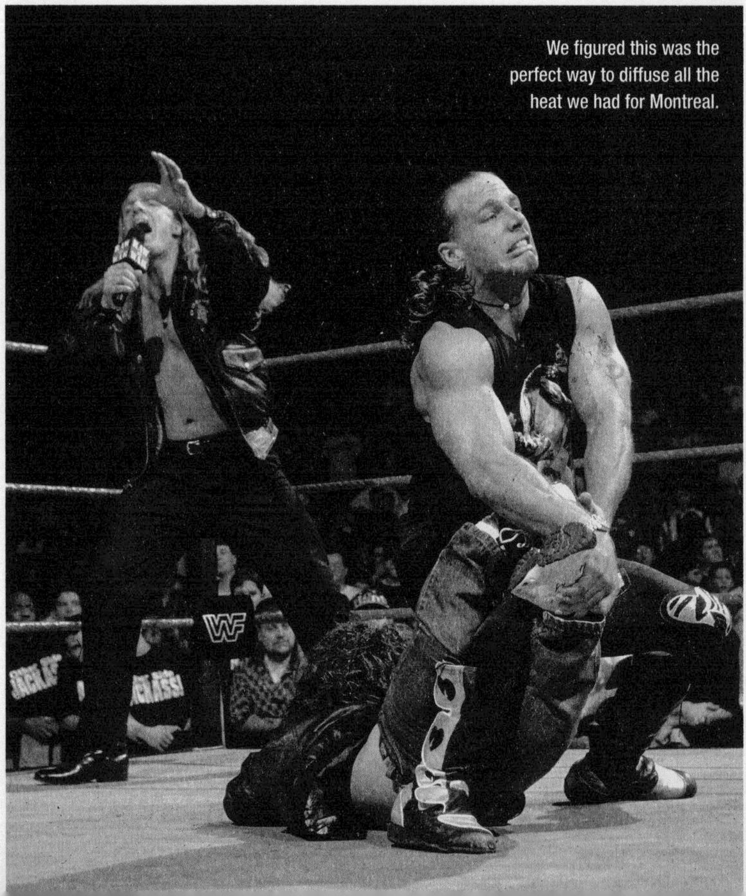

We figured this was the perfect way to diffuse all the heat we had for Montreal.

HUNTER: November 9, 1997, will probably go down as one of, if not the, most significant date in the history of the business; more important than April 3, 1908, when Frank Gotch defeated George Hackenschmidt in the "match of the century"; more important than May 17, 1963, when Bruno Sammartino defeated Buddy Rogers and ushered in the predominance of World Wide Wrestling Federation; more important than January 23, 1984, when Hulk Hogan defeated the Iron Sheik.

SHAWN: And more important than July 6, 2000, when the Brooklyn Brawler beat Triple H.

HUNTER: Or how about February 27, 2006, when Shawn Michaels joined Vince McMahon's Kiss My Ass Club?

SHAWN: While the debate over who was right and who was wrong concerning what went on in Montreal will probably linger forever, some will always take Bret's side, some will take mine and Vince's, but the profound impact of the match changed the direction of the industry forever.

HUNTER: In the immediate aftermath of the controversy, Vince abandoned his television announcer role and introduced the world to the Mr. McMahon character, and you could say that WWE officially entered The Attitude Era. It's no coincidence that soon after, Vince took over the industry and vanquished WCW. It also made us even more unpopular than we already were. Being who we were, we saw it as an opportunity to push boundaries even further. The result was greater ratings, greater heat, and even more trouble backstage.

When the crap with Bret happened, we had so much heat. The fans hated us, so many of the boys hated us. After the match, we had to run across the street through a mob scene to get back to our hotel. I even got punched in the face.

Now, there were a few guys in the back who backed us up and said they would be there with us, but there weren't a lot. It became so fricken tense every night. I remember one night we were in Worcester and we were walking up a hallway. We had just finished working and there were some kids from a local hockey team walking toward us. They looked like they were tough kids. We were really on edge, and one of the kids said, "Hey, we watch you guys on TV!" I stuck my hand out to shake hands, and the kid turned around and stuck his hand out. Shawn just saw a hand coming at me out of the corner of his eye and grabbed the kid and started to pull him off me like he was attacking me. It was just so edgy. We were teetering on the brink all the time.

SHAWN: Because we just didn't know. We didn't know at the time. We didn't know who was going to jump out of the woodwork and attack us. And it was pretty tense here in general at the time. The other company was still beating us in the ratings and seemed to have everyone on edge. Everyone was feeling pressure and it was just intense. And with us on top it was really weird because the more heat there was, the more gasoline we poured on it.

HUNTER: All we needed was a spark to let it go off, and we just kept adding more fuel.

SHAWN: Nobody realized that the more uptight they got, the more they were egging us on. The more upset they got, the more they whined, the harder we pressed. I mean, Hunter got punished for a year and it is not in his nature to show anger. I wondered if he saw it as his chance to get back.

HUNTER: It was, but at the same point in time, there was something empowering about what we were doing. Usually when people do stupid stuff, they do more of it with someone else than they would do on their own. It was an opportunity for me to stick it to everybody, but also to do something that I felt was right for the business. Because I had a partner in crime, it made it a whole lot easier to go out there and say "F the world." I had somebody next to me saying "F the world," and if you don't like it I had someone standing next to me saying "Hell, we'll fight you."

SHAWN: That's true. It was the two of us, and no one else was on our side. We both were going to take it on the chin and ride it out and sink or swim. I'm just thankful that I had such a good friend standing with me. That's not something you have a lot in this line of work.

HUNTER: It got to the point where Shawn and I had hand signals worked out in case someone tried to turn one of Shawn's matches into a real shoot. If things turned into a shoot, he'd flash a hand signal and I'd hit the ring and start kicking ass. They might beat us up, but they'd get a hell of a fight with both of us. That's the point we had reached after Montreal. The first time we did it was when Shawn wrestled Ken Shamrock at the DX Pay-Per-View in December. I remember talking about it. Shamrock may be the world's most dangerous man, but he can't take both of us. Shawn would give me the hand sign, and I'd come running to the ring and clobber him.

Shamrock was real good friends with Bret. And even though he had come to us and said, "What you guys did was business, and I got no problem with you," how did we not know that this was the setup?

SHAWN: We couldn't trust anyone.

HUNTER: We trusted each other, and that was it.

SHAWN: Sometimes it was an issue getting to and from the ring. It was dicey. The heat we were getting was real.

HUNTER: The one thing is that we weren't afraid of it. And I don't mean for this to sound like a cocky thing. If we were walking across the street and someone flipped us off, we flipped them off right back. There was no, "Let's go to a hotel and hide."

SHAWN: We had each other and we were fine. The same thing for the dressing room. It wasn't like we were a bunch of wallflowers. The other thing is that I was too angry to worry.

HUNTER: All that mattered to me was that when the music would hit and we would walk out, the place would go crazy. We caused back-to-back riots in Memphis and Little Rock. What happened in Memphis was that we were supposed to work in a tag match with Jerry Lawler & Jeff Jarrett. The fans were throwing so much stuff when we were about to go out there that it was deemed unsafe.

Then the next night in Little Rock, we were going to lock up with Shamrock & Danny Hodge. Hodge was going to beat us up, but it never happened. There was a huge riot. There was a fire in the building and people were fighting near the ring. The police told us it was all our fault and surrounded us with cop cars. They drove us to the city line and said don't come back. I couldn't go to Little Rock till just a few years ago when I helped open up the new building there.

We believed we were doing the best thing for the business. The rest of the locker room might not have agreed, but they couldn't deny the crowd reaction we were getting. Nobody in the business had talked about causing riots for years.

SHAWN: That was serious Old School heat. I guess that was one Old School quality we didn't mind keeping. People were hating us like nothing we'd seen before. But that's the reaction we wanted.

HUNTER: Another funny thing that happened in Little Rock is that it was close to Christmas, and we decided to get a case of beer and stick it in the locker room with a sign that said "Merry Christmas, DX." We weren't trying to kiss ass, but we weren't all bad, and we figured let's make a little peace offering. And then of course we cause a riot and the building gets set on fire.

SHAWN: It's almost like we were Homer Simpson trying to do something good and it still blew up in our faces.

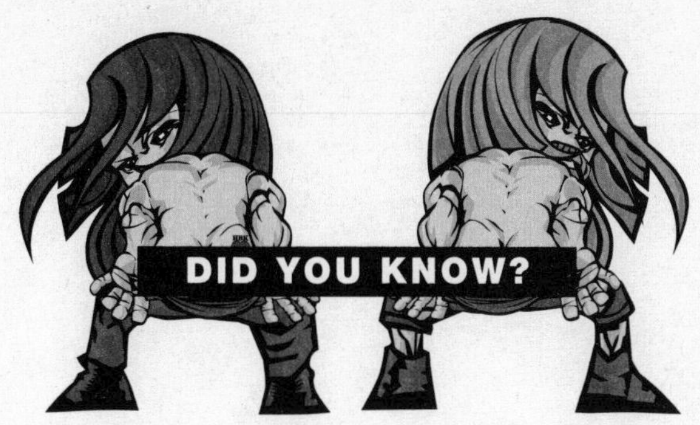

The night after *Survivor Series*, we debuted the D-Generation X theme song.

HUNTER: We had a lot of input into our theme music. We told them we wanted a Rage Against the Machine type song, and they tried several times to come up with songs for us. But none of them really fit what we were about. Finally they got Chris Warren and his band to perform "Break It Down." Vince played it for us in his office, and I knew instantly that this was it.

R.I.P.
IN THE WWF
EUROPEAN CHAMPION

MATCH OF THE CENTURY

SHAWN MICHAELS

"This is not an easy thing to be defeated for the coveted European title. I've been in Ladder and Hell in a Cell matches, Marathon matches, but never has any match been so emotionally and physically draining as this one."

TRIPLE H

"I'd just like to say one thing: That other than my kid being born, and I don't have one that I know of, but this is the greatest moment of my life. Yo Sarge, I did it! I did it!"

HUNTER: Sgt. Slaughter finally thought he could put one over on us by making Shawn defend his European title against me. We, of course, had other ideas . . .

SHAWN: If there ever was a moment that was sure to anger the so-called wrestling purists, it was the European

Championship match between myself and Hunter. For a "grueling" one minute and seventeen seconds, we pulled on the ropes, circled each other, and refused to lock up. When we finally locked up, I dropped like a sack of bricks. Hunter proceeded to run the ropes like the biggest goon in the world.

With J.R. yelling, "This is a mockery! This is a mockery!" Triple H covered me for the win. Triple H celebrated as if his boyhood dream had come true. Jim Cornette, who was commenting with J.R. at the time, could only yell, "It was a ruse, a plot, a mockery, a sham! We've been conned, bamboozled! Look at those jackasses!"

We were too friendly for people to believe we would fight for the title. When we told people what we wanted to do instead of having a real match, they were all up in arms. "You are going to expose the business" all over again. But it was so far over the top, everyone knew it was an act.

HUNTER: It took us all day to get the powers to buy in to it. A lot of people were upset even when we got the OK.

SHAWN: That was the thing: The more we did these kinds of things, the more people would get hot when we came to the back. We would get in trouble, but after a while they began to hear the reaction of the crowds and the heat we were generating.

HUNTER: We didn't get fined. Well, I know I didn't get fined because I didn't have any money then. It was just verbal heat: "You can't do that!" What the hell are you doing? They are going to take us off the air!" That was Vince and the agents telling us this. The agents would come to us under the guise of trying to help us, and they would try to reason with us. We didn't change, though, because we thought what we were doing was good and so did the fans.

There was also a bit of us that just didn't care. And I hate to say that because some of the young guys now will say, "How did you not care?" Well, we cared so much that we didn't care. We truly believed that stuff was good, no matter what. And that's how we felt. We didn't give a crap about what happened to us because we cared so much about the business.

SHAWN: We really felt that that was where the business was going. We weren't out to insult anybody. We really felt that we were not saying anything different than people sitting at home watching TV were thinking.

The European title mockery was so far over the top it was ridiculous. I mean, you have to look at the silliness. All the traditional stuff that everyone found so sacred, we [World Wrestling Federation] were the only ones defending it. Everyone knew. It's just stupid.

HUNTER: The proof was that despite how much we were hated, people wanted to work with us. No matter how much you hate someone, if he's going to put food on your table, you know you are going to work with him. When we were working with Undertaker, someone said, "Boy, I hate Shawn, but look how he made Undertaker look like a million bucks. I wish I could have a match like that with him. I hate him, but if I can have a match like that and he can make me look like that, then screw it, I want to work with him." I think that's the mentality of the boys. I don't think a lot of the guys liked Hogan, but they wanted to work with him.

SHAWN: We might have got the best of people in promos, but for the most part, we both got beat up in the ring. It always took the two of us and Chyna to get to our opponents, and that made them look stronger.

HUNTER: They call that wiener dogging. We're not real big, but if there's a pack of us, we can get you down. When the matches were taking place, we were making everyone else look good. Mostly we just got the crap kicked out of us at house shows. We got beat up and embarrassed. And that's another reason others wanted to work with us, because we were giving it all back to our opponents. We were like bouncing balls, ping, ping, ping, ping. We were doing all this crazy stuff to get heat, and the crowd either loved it or hated it, and then we would bounce all over the place and make our opponents look good. What's not to like, and why wouldn't you want to work with us?

DISCRETION IS ADVISED BUT WILL BE COMPLETELY IGNORED

JIM ROSS

"Oh good Lord, ladies and gentlemen, I apologize!"

HUNTER: A large part of our success can be attributed to our willingness to talk about the back side of the business on television. But we would not have been nearly as successful if that's all we did.

We were rebels, but we were obnoxious and angry. Steve Austin was being a rebel at the same time, but he was much more serious than we were. We rebelled by acting like jerk-offs.

SHAWN: On the December 8, 1997, *Raw,* the creative staff asked us to play poker in the ring while we waited for Owen Hart to come out . . .

HUNTER: That was a no-brainer. They told us about the idea to play poker and it was another thing that we just ran with. Shawn was half in the bag by the time we went after the Headbangers. Not the right thing to do, obviously, but remember, Shawn was an angry young man at the time. This scene was typical for us. Somebody would come up with a concept that we were supposed to do for TV that week, and we would just run with it.

SHAWN: We would go way far with it. Creative had handed me a Jack Daniel's bottle that was filled with tea. I threw that out and had someone get me a real bottle of Jack Daniel's, which I drank throughout the poker game. Hunter had some, but he slowed down when he realized we were drinking the real thing.

HUNTER: It wasn't disorganized chaos, it was more like organized chaos. We were out there, but there was control and an idea to get where we were going. If they said the line was here, we went past the line. We went really far past the line, but all for the right reasons as far as we were concerned.

SHAWN: We were constantly going over things. Any subject that was brought up could spark an idea. We both had long hair, so we decided to do something different with it. We braided it and I started whacking people with it. It was stupid and annoying, but funny.

HUNTER: In the lead-up to Shawn's Casket match against Undertaker at *Royal Rumble,* we decided to hold a little "Undertaker Barbecue." We burned his clothes, made fun of his use of fire, and, of course, got off numerous "weenie" jokes.

SHAWN: It's just juvenile. But what person hasn't been at a barbecue and made a stupid joke like that? We took it so far over the top you had to laugh.

HUNTER: Everyone else was being so serious and we were just being jack-offs. And that was the thing. A lot of time when we went on TV we didn't know what we were going to say, my radar was just up looking for the most ludicrous thing I could say. If I could make Shawn laugh, I could make anyone laugh, and that was the goal.

Not what Creative expected.

RAW
WAR

Merry Christmas, ladies!

A FUNNY THING HAPPENS ALONG THE WAY

HUNTER: Traditionally speaking, we had been consistently positioned as heels. We broke rules, disrespected authority, and cheated and made fun of opponents whenever the opportunity arose. Our actions made us the most hated trio in World Wrestling Federation.

As we carried on and kept getting more and more outrageous, however, some people just couldn't hate us anymore. We were funny and cool, and in this business at that time, it was tough to stay hated when you are perceived that way. People who started off screaming and booing at us, they started to like us. It started slowly, but before long, entire sections of fans started cheering for us. The reason? We were entertaining the hell out of them.

SHAWN: It was weird at first. We were doing everything from a heel perspective, but what happened was we got so over the top and so edgy that fans started liking us.

HUNTER: The world had changed to the point where ten years prior if guys had that kind of heat they could maintain that. At this point in time, when you got that much heat, people would start digging you. There was a large segment of the population that said, "That's really cool. Those guys don't give a damn about what they say or do." And that's when we started going from people throwing crap at us to girls throwing their underwear or flipping their boobs out, or guys, instead of coming at us to kill us, guys started coming at us to tell us we are the shit.

It was in Springfield, Massachusetts, at the DX Pay-Per-View, that I noticed we were getting really popular. I mean, when girls start flashing their boobs, it's like, take notice. And the girls and their boyfriends had made shirts with DX all over them. These people were really into us. It was different, because I don't remember seeing that before, somebody making the effort to make a shirt. Seeing that made us bolder. We were saying F-U to you guys in the back, and now the fans are saying F-U to you guys too.

SHAWN: It continued to snowball and the ratings were going up and nothing backfired. It just kept getting bigger and bigger in every aspect.

HUNTER: There's a certain part, like when we went out in those Christmas thongs. Whether you hated us or thought it was the gayest stuff of all time, you almost have to respect two guys who write Merry Xmas on their butts. They had to be thinking these guys are kind of out there. I think there were some times where stuff we were doing wasn't all done in anger but done just to amuse ourselves, and everyone else was thinking it was funny too.

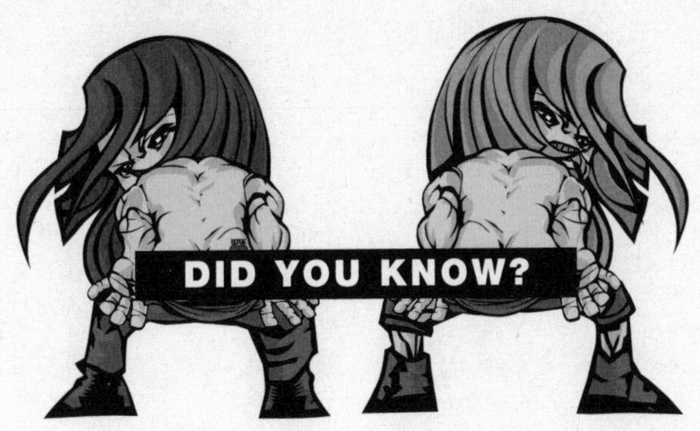

On September 22, 1997, the Brooklyn Brawler won a Battle Royal at Madison Square Garden to win a title shot the next time World Wrestling Federation came to the World's Most Famous Arena. When the company returned on November 15, 1997, Shawn Michaels was champion. Brawler nearly defeated Shawn, getting a two-and-a-half count at one point. To this day, Brawler believes he should have won that match, and if he had, he would have taken control of DX and led it to even greater fame and fortune.

RAW
IS
WAR

THE GREAT BETRAYAL

SHAWN MICHAELS

"And what I am doing right now is treating you like a man. But make no mistake about Mike. I am calling your ass out right now, right here. Boy!"

MIKE TYSON

"You want to do it?"

SHAWN: In January 1998, Vince brought former Heavyweight Boxing Champion, the self-proclaimed "Baddest Man on the Planet," Mike Tyson, to World Wrestling Federation. Tyson was to be the special guest enforcer during the championship match between myself and Stone Cold Steve Austin at *WrestleMania XIV*.

At first Tyson teased that he was going to be partial to Austin, but we had something in the works, and in a shocking turnaround, he ended up joining DX and torturing Stone Cold with us in the weeks and days leading up to *WrestleMania*.

At *WrestleMania*, Tyson turned on us and counted the

one-two-three on me after Austin gave me the Stunner. To add insult to injury, he then knocked me out after I started to berate him for turning on us

HUNTER: It was really cool to work with Mike. Shawn was very, very angry at that time. That was his peak of stress. But we were all Tyson fans, and I can remember one time racing after a show to a sports bar to try and see him fight.

My biggest recollection with him was when we did the reveal, when Mike joined us. Shawn pulled the shirt off of him, and he had the DX shirt on. I just remember Tyson giggling like a little kid, and he kept walking by and saying, "This is so cool, this is so cool," and then yelling, "Suck it!" and "This is so much fun!"

SHAWN: Mike was really into it. I remember that much.

HUNTER: He was a huge fan and he loved DX and he thought we were the coolest thing in the world. Just being around him was fun. I remember when we had the special DX workout at Government Center in Boston right before *WrestleMania XIV*. Shawn and Mike were going over the stuff they were going to say, and I thought I had better listen to this, so I did. It's a good thing I did.

We thought it would be this little thing. We had no idea there were going to be thousands of people there. We were driving through this huge crowd to get there and there were people as far as you could see. So we finally get there and we get in the ring. People were yelling at us and throwing stuff at us. We were getting hit. These people were really pissed off at us. We had turned on Austin and he was white hot. So we are there getting yelled at, and Shawn gets hit with a battery. Shawn was already in a bad mood and just got fed up and said he was out of here and left.

I watched him walk to the car and slam the door, and I thought to myself, "He ain't coming back." I turned and I looked out and there were thirty thousand people looking at us, and Tyson turns to me and asks, "What are we going to do now?"

Just before *WrestleMania XIV,* kicking Stone Cold's ass.

I said, "Good question."

Joanie then told me that Shawn wasn't coming back. I said, "He'll be back when Austin's here. He won't miss the publicity shot. He's just not going to do all warm-up stuff."

Sure enough, when Steve arrived, Shawn came back and we were able to go through the program and get in the news.

Personally, I didn't care what the angle was with them. In order to get face time, I would just stand next to Mike whenever cameras were around, and I'd get in the shot. I knew he was getting the publicity . . .

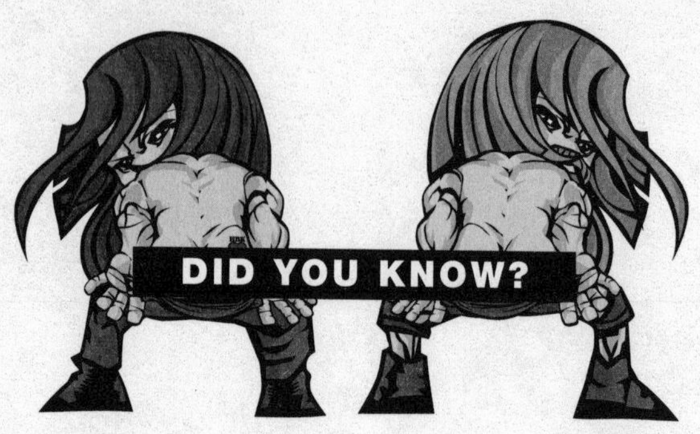

The DX Band purposely butchered the National Anthem at the beginning of *WrestleMania XIV* in order to generate more heat toward Shawn and Hunter.

HUNTER: One of my best memories of *WrestleMania XIV* is the DX Band. We brought Chris Warren and his band in to play live. They were so jazzed to be there, and when they played the National Anthem, Shawn and I couldn't get enough of it. I remember thinking those guys just butchered that song, that's awesome! Everyone else was really hot, saying it was sacrilegious to destroy the National Anthem. We just laughed, and that, of course, pissed people off even more.

DX

RAW
WAR

LOOKING BACK

HUNTER: We were the two guys who opened the doors. Everyone else was still behind the door and keeping it closed as to where you could go in the business. We didn't peek through, we didn't look through, we kicked the door and everyone followed us. That, to me, is what we did. We were the two guys who had the balls to do it.

SHAWN: There aren't many things from a wrestling standpoint that you can do that are really fresh. And we were able to do them. That will last forever in this business. There are so few firsts, and we were part of the initial breakthrough. Also, though, we made it fun. I think we made wrestling fun again, or we had a large part in that, and that's something I'm proud of.

HUNTER: I hear people say "revolutionize the business," but we did that by making the business fun. We made it fun whether you hated us and wanted your favorite guys to beat us up, or whether you liked us because it was fun to watch these guys who are such tools that you couldn't help but laugh at them. Either way, we made it fun again to watch wrestling. How we got it to be fun was a different story, but we made it fun to watch.

SHAWN: Things were so tense most of the time, it wasn't like we were having fun in the sense of sitting around laughing all the time. The fun came more from being innovative and doing new things. Making a difference is fun. Many people thought we were being disrespectful to the business, but it was the complete opposite. We have great respect for this business. We just wanted to bring in something fresh.

In retrospect, we helped change the entire landscape of the business, and that's fun. To be a part of something new and fresh is fun. When we were going through it we had all the emotions, good and bad, but looking back and seeing how it turned out, we can sit back and smile. At the time there was the question, "Was it the right thing to do?" Looking back, I think everyone will say, "Yes." But remember, back in 1997, there were only two guys who were saying "change," and that's Hunter and myself. Any time you are right it's fun.

HUNTER: I think if you'd have asked us at the time, "Are you having fun doing that?" despite the laughing, I don't think we would have said, "Hey, that was really fun." We were coming from an angry place. While we were laughing and stuff, there was a lot of intensity behind it.

SHAWN: I think the laughing came from that we stuck it to someone.

THE FUTURE OF DX

SHAWN: I really didn't know what the future held for me after *WrestleMania XIV*. As far as DX was concerned, we had done all the heavy lifting. DX had worked, and our philosophy had proved successful. One thing for sure was that Hunter wasn't going to have to go through all the heat that we got for doing what we believed in. DX was a presence now.

HUNTER: The problem for me was that DX was over, but no matter how you cut it, Shawn was the main guy. I was the second guy, the second fiddle. My concern was to be able to step up and take his role. It was going to be up to me to see if there were legs to this group.

SHAWN: Long before *WrestleMania*, we had thought about adding Billy Gunn and Road Dogg to the group.

HUNTER: We had gone to Vince early on and said, "You are not doing anything with Billy and Road Dogg. Make them a tag team. Let them start to go on their own, start to get over, and when the time is right we'll bring them in." We wanted to bring them in when they were over so we would have more over guys. But it was important to let them be together first and let them get over on their own, not something that came out of DX. When they started getting over so well on their own, we were like, "Those guys don't need us. Let them stay on their own as long as they need to." When Shawn left it was the perfect time for them to join for a bunch of reasons.

SHAWN: We had done things on TV mentoring them, but they didn't need to come in and join us before *WrestleMania*.

HUNTER: When Shawn left, we, DX, really needed them. DX is no good if it's just me.

SHAWN: Truthfully, I wasn't in any kind of mind to make thoughtful decisions. I didn't know what would have made sense to me at that point.

ACT TWO

I SAID, ARE YOU READY?

THE PLAYERS

D-GENERATION X

Triple H: a.k.a. Hunter Hearst-Helmsley; Hunter. The leader of the DX Army. Known for his quick wit, ring psychology, and exceptionally large genitalia.

The Crock: A strange hybrid of Triple H and The Rock who likes to smell what he's been baking in the men's room.

Chyna: a.k.a. the Ninth Wonder of the World. Still known for beating up male Superstars and increasing her breast size.

Road Dogg: a.k.a. Brian Armstrong; Roadie; Jesse James. One half of the New Age Outlaws and, according to Triple H, one of the funniest people on the planet.

B'Lo: A curious-looking wrestler who can't stop shaking and shimmying and likes to repeat everything The Crock says.

Billy Gunn: a.k.a. Mr. Ass; Rockabilly. The other half of the New Age Outlaws. Would later go on to achieve great fame by participating in WWE's first and only commitment ceremony.

X-Pac: a.k.a. the 1-2-3 Kid; Syxx. Original Kliq member who joins DX, leaves DX, beats Shane McMahon, loses to Shane McMahon, and forms a peculiar friendship with Kane.

Mizark: A genetic experiment gone wrong that produces an X-Pac/Mark Henry hybrid.

OTHER PLAYERS

Cactus Jack: A rough-and-tumble brawler from Truth or Consequences, New Mexico, who bears a striking resemblance to Mankind and Dude Love. Tag team partner of Chainsaw Charlie.

Chainsaw Charlie: a.k.a. Hoss Funk, a.k.a. Terry Funk; the Funkster. Hardcore legend who teams up with Cactus Jack.

Colonel Woody: DX's fearless tank/jeep driver, who continues on with his mission, no matter the danger.

Eric Bischoff: Boss of WCW, whom DX humiliates over and over again.

WCW Fans: People who would much rather watch DX and World Wrestling Federation, but since Eric Bischoff gives them free tickets, they come to WCW shows.

Michael Buffer: Famous ring announcer who sounds a lot like Triple H.

Disciples of Apocalypse: A rough-and-tumble biker faction. DX pees on their motorcycles just for kicks.

The Rock: a.k.a. the Great One; Rocky Maivia. Cohort and rival of Triple H's whose charisma and talent help bring out the best in Triple H.

Hulk Hogan: a.k.a. the Hulkster; Sterling Golden; Hulk Machine. Aging and balding Superstar.

Mark Henry: a.k.a. World's Strongest Man; Sexual Chocolate. Former Olympic weightlifter and member of The Nation who becomes strangely addicted to Chyna.

The Nation: A faction comprised of The Rock, Mark Henry, D'Lo Brown, The Godfather, and Owen Hart. Despite all the talent in this faction, they are best known for being made fun of by DX.

Kane: Undertaker's tormented younger brother who likes to light people on fire.

The Corporation: Vince McMahon's organization that at one point or another seemingly includes everyone on the World Wrestling Federation roster, as well as McMahon's stooges. Through the Corporation, Mr. McMahon attempts to exert total control over World Wrestling Federation.

Test: A poor humiliated sap who has his bride stolen away by Triple H the night before his wedding.
Stephanie McMahon: a.k.a. the Billionaire Princess. The apple of Mr. McMahon's eye, who proves to have great taste in men and be a lot smarter than her dad.
Shane McMahon: a.k.a. Shane O Mac. Son of Vince McMahon who trades the European title back and forth with X-Pac.
Dick Cheatem: Turner executive who allows DX to infiltrate the CNN center in Atlanta, Georgia.

SHAWN: Hey, Hunter, I just looked, and I see I'm not on the list of players in this act.
HUNTER: Well, Shawn, you remember you needed some time away to heal your body and clear your mind.
SHAWN: I vaguely seem to remember something like that going on. So what you're saying is that I'm not really needed here for a while?
HUNTER: Why don't you go grab an ice cold soda and relax. I'll call you back when we need you. You did make a few guest appearances during the next few years.
SHAWN: OK. But before I go, I just want to make sure all our readers know about all the great DX merchandise available on WWEShop.com.
HUNTER: OK, Shawn. Why don't you tell them about all the great DX merchandise available on WWEShop.com.
SHAWN: We have a lot of great merchandise available on WWEShop.com. T-shirts, hats, sweatshirts, shorts, backpacks, DVDs, clocks, magnets—you name it, we got it. And the great thing is that WWEShop.com is open twenty-four hours a day, so you don't have to worry about pulling yourself away from the book right now. You can listen to Triple H talk about this time period for DX and then check out the merchandise later. I don't remember all the details from this period because I was kind of out of it and away from WWE, but I do recollect that DX did some pretty wacky stuff.
HUNTER: Thanks, Shawn, for that shameless plug for DX merchandise on WWEShop.com. Now back to our story . . .

RAW
IS
WAR

THE DX ARMY

TRIPLE H

"You know, a lot can happen in twenty-four hours. Let's start with Mike Tyson. I must have asked a thousand times, 'Is he locked in? Is he with us? Are you sure? Is it sewn up?'

"What I heard was, 'Don't worry, kid, I got it covered, don't sweat it. Let me make the decisions.' Well, you dropped the ball. But don't worry, HBK, because Triple H picked it up and now the ball is in my court! I'll take care of the worries, I'll take care of the problems, and I'll make the decisions!

"This is the genesis of D-Generation X. Tonight, live, in front of the world, I form the DX Army. An army to take care of business that should have been taken care of right from the start. And when you start an army, when you set out to start what no one else can do, the first thing you do is you look to your blood. You look to your buddies, you look to your friends, you look to The Kliq."

JIM ROSS

"Well look who's back . . . a new day is dawning for DX."

HUNTER: The day following *WrestleMania XIV*, Shawn went home to Texas. He had a severely injured back and didn't know if he'd ever be able to wrestle again. The future of D-Generation X lay squarely on my shoulders. Its success was very much in doubt . . .

When Shawn went home after *WrestleMania*, I believed that I could keep DX successful, but I think there were a lot of people who thought I couldn't do it on my own. Sometimes the hardest thing to do in this business is convince people that you have the ability to get the job done. It's very hard to actually get the chance to prove yourself.

I don't think they thought about not giving me the chance. I think Vince was pretty adamant about giving me the opportunity, but I was pretty sure that a lot of people thought this thing would die. And maybe they had a point. In reality, Shawn was *the* catalyst for DX. He was the bigger star and the top guy. I was more or less his sidekick during the previous run.

I definitely felt the pressure the first night after *WrestleMania*. We were in Albany, New York, and it was made very clear that I needed to hit a home run that first night. I knew that if I didn't make it happen immediately, DX would never be what it could be. It was huge now, and if I let it die in one week, DX could never recover. I knew bringing out X-Pac and Billy and Road Dogg would definitely help, but it was also on me. I was the original guy. I had to be the catalyst for those guys. I was very nervous, excited about the chance, but definitely very nervous because of what was at stake.

I really believed that Kid was going to be important to our success, and I fought hard to bring him back to the company. Many people were like, "Screw him, he's not money." But I felt we really needed a spark. We had Billy and Road Dogg, but we still needed something else. Kid was hot coming out of nWo and getting fired from WCW. Plus, people knew that we were friends from The Kliq days, and that had a life of its own.

I wasn't one hundred percent sure he was coming in until the week it actually happened. They told me, and I was like, "Thank God." It would have been hard without him. We needed something special that first night out there.

The plan was for me to talk some stuff about Shawn and then bring Kid out. When Kid came out, there was this huge positive reaction. Toward the end of the run with Shawn, there were groups of people who had started liking us, but when Kid came out it was on a whole different level.

I think the combination of me talking bad about Shawn and then Kid crapping on WCW, Hulk Hogan, and Eric Bischoff made us really cool in the fans' eyes. I could sense that we were on to something different here. Because the crowd reaction was so great, I wasn't sure whether we were going to be heels. I was thinking the fans might really start to like us, but I felt we had to go down that heel route in order to make it authentic.

When Kid, Chyna, and I interfered in the Outlaws' match against Cactus Jack & Chainsaw Charlie, the fans didn't get on us. Again, we were perceived as something cool rather than heels. The fans really weren't hot at us. We all knew that the show was a great success for us and that we might really be on to something different than had come before.

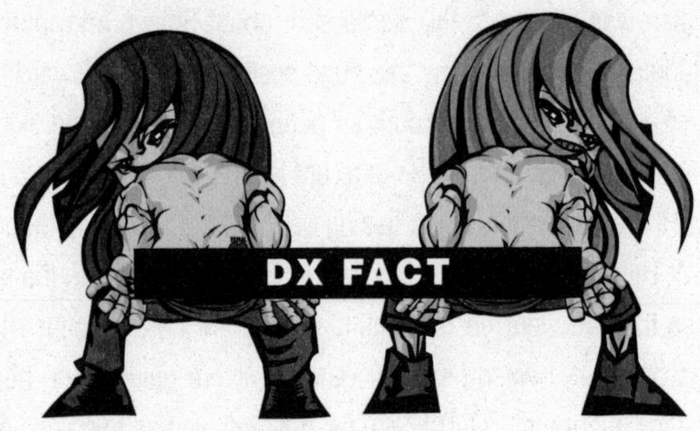

One of the first things we did in this version of DX was pee on the DOA's motorcycles. The creative team told us that they wanted us to do something to DOA [Disciples of Apocalypse] to tick them off. It was our idea to pee on them. After all, if you wanted to get them angry by doing something to their bikes, you can't do much better than peeing on them.

Now I've been asked, "Did you guys really pee on them?" Let me put it to you this way: When we found out what we were going to do, we went straight to catering and started drinking all the water we could. Some of us, I won't say who, managed to get our hands on a few cold ones as well. If you watch the videotape of the incident, you'll see that we were peeing for quite a while, and they only showed a small part of the time we were near the bikes. We were later told that the bikes had a couple of grand in damage that had to be fixed. The mechanic said the engines looked like they had been saturated in salty water.

D-GENERATION X

THE INVASION

TRIPLE H

"Atteeeeention! Today we embark on a mission. We have seen the enemy, and they are near. This mission will start at the Norfolk Scope with WCW rasslin'!

"D-Generation X, the only group with the cajones big enough, proudly starts the war against WCW. Ladies and gentlemen, do you think Eric Bischoff sucks?"

WCW FANS

"Yes!"

TRIPLE H

"What I'd like to know is that, from experience, not what you think, does WCW suck?"

WCW FANS

"Of course!"

TRIPLE H

"Who rules in professional wrestling?"

WCW FANS

"DX! DX!"

HUNTER: The invasion of WCW at the Norfolk Scope was without a doubt one of the biggest and best things DX ever did. Nobody knew anything about that from the DX side except for me. At that time, WCW was doing something that was not necessarily the best thing for their business, but what they thought was the best thing to do to hurt our business.

When they saw us book a show somewhere, they would go and try to book a competing show as close as possible to where we were. For example, if we scheduled a show at the the Rose Garden in Virginia Beach, they would book a show at the Norfolk Scope the same night.

So I was on a phone call with Vince McMahon and Vince Russo, our head writer, and we were talking about this. Somebody said, "You know what? Those guys are doing a show at the Scope right down the street from us."

It really pissed us off, and I made some offhanded comment to the effect that I'd really like to just go down there and mess with their show or something like that. I just said it off the cuff, and five minutes later Vince Russo asked, "Why can't we do that?" From there, this idea just started mushrooming, and the more we talked about it, the more I thought that this was going to be unbelievable.

When we got to our arena that day and I saw all the army props around, I still didn't know exactly what we were going to do. The original concept was to get a full-blown tank and ride it down the street. We couldn't do that though, because a tank would have torn up the roads, so we ended up with the jeep with the cannon on the back.

Billy and Dogg got to the show a bit later, and Billy came up to me and asked, "What's all that army stuff out there? Is it for us? I saw them painting a big X on it."

Now, Vince had told me not to tell anybody about our plans because if word got out the whole project would fail. So I said, "I can't tell you what it is, but believe me, it's going to be awesome."

When I finally told them what we were going to do, they were like, "Holy crap! We're gonna do what?"

So I said, "We are going to take that jeep with the cannon and drive down to the Scope and declare war. We are going to try and actually go in the building and interrupt their show."

They just couldn't believe it. All sorts of questions started flying, and someone said, "Here's the one thing that we didn't think of. Their show is on first, before ours. What happens if they then decide to grab all their guys and come down and screw up our show?" And Vince said, "Open the doors and let them in. What show are you going to watch? The one with all the wrestlers on it or the one with no wrestlers on it?" This was when I really came to appreciate how smart Vince was. WCW, of course, didn't think that way. When we got there, they locked the doors on us. If they were smart, they would have let us in. Imagine the interest if DX invaded their show and they let it run. The ratings would have been huge, and they probably could have humiliated us given that they controlled the production.

So when it was time to get going, we still had no idea what we were actually going to do. We parked a few blocks away, shot a little vignette where we talked about invading WCW, and then just set off for the Scope.

Their show was close to starting when we made our way there. Fans were coming in. As soon as we started coming down the street, fans starting seeing us, and they couldn't believe we were there. They were just eating us up. The funny thing is, we still had no idea what we were going to do once we got to the building. We had a bullhorn and the cannon, and that's all we knew. We just went out, and I declared war on WCW and fired the first shot from the cannon. Of course, when I tried to fire the gun and pulled the chain, nothing happened. We all just started laughing.

Nobody even mentioned WCW. Back then WCW didn't even exist in the WWE world until we drove that jeep up and shot a F***ing cannon at it. We didn't walk through the door, we *blew* the doors off.

When we started with Shawn we opened up the business to the point where people in the back said, "How can they let those guys say that?" But as babyfaces now, we opened up the business to what it really was. Everyone knew about WCW, we needed to talk about it on this show.

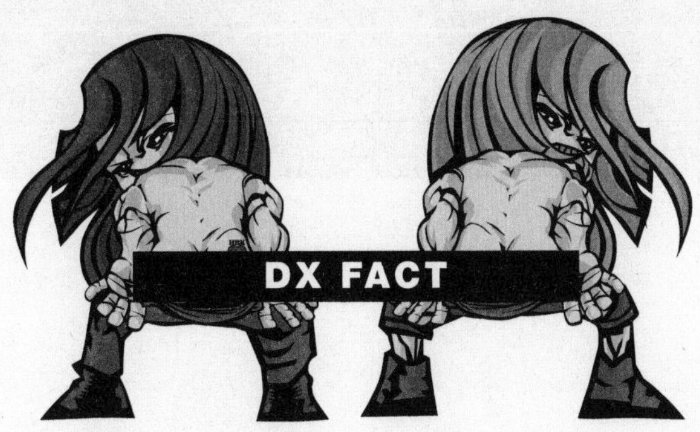

Colonel Woody was not a World Wrestling Federation employee. He ran the prop shop where DX rented the jeep and said that he had to drive the jeep. Little did he know he would become a sports entertainment legend one day—or at least an answer to an obscure wrestling trivia question.

THE BATTLE RAGES ON

TRIPLE H

"Did you pay for your ticket to come here tonight?"

FAN

"Hell no! I got 'em for free!"

TRIPLE H

"D-Generation X will now visit the box office to see if there are any more of the free tickets that they try to give away to fill up their TV every week."

HUNTER: As we made our way to the building, the fans started going crazy. They were clamoring all around us, playing off us. It couldn't have started out any better.

Then we saw the big electronic billboard out front. It was announcing all the upcoming events, and there was a sign for some kind of rodeo that was coming up. It listed the name and date, and then the screen flashed, "Free Tickets Available."

Right afterward came the sign for WCW. So when you watched the billboard, it looked like it was saying free tickets available for WCW *Nitro.* We filmed it and just edited out the first part about the rodeo. What viewers saw was "Free tickets available for WCW *Nitro.*" It looked like they had to give away tickets to get people there. We saw the opportunity and struck.

We started asking fans—and mind you, we weren't prompting anyone—but we asked them where they got their tickets, and many straight out said that they got them free from a radio station or some other person, and it just played out perfectly for us.

The one mistake we made was that we should have tried to go into the building first and then do all the other stuff, because by the time we got to the building they knew we were there and they locked the doors so we couldn't get inside.

When I got back to our building, there was a message on my phone from Kevin Nash. He left it as he was riding to the Scope in his car. "I don't know what's going on, but I just pulled up to our building and you guys are outside shooting at our building, that's awesome!" He was laughing. Then he left me another message explaining what had gone on inside the building.

WCW used to call their production meeting "the War Room" because it was "war" against *Raw.* So Kev walked into the War Room and everyone was acting as if nothing special was going on. They had no idea what we were doing. Kevin looked at them strangely and asked, "That doesn't bother you guys?" And they were like, "What doesn't bother us?"

Then Kev told them that DX is outside shooting at the building, with masses of fans cheering for them. They were like, "What?" And they started losing it. That's when they locked the doors.

It's too bad we didn't get inside, because who knows what would have happened. We had all these contingency plans set up. We had a fake camera and bogus tapes in case they tried to confiscate our equipment.

We also had a plan that if Bischoff came out and even slightly touched me—or if anyone touched me, for that matter—I would go down like I had a heart attack to distract everyone, and our cameraman would change the bogus tapes for the real ones and then take off. It was pretty exciting. I really wonder how it all would have played out if we got inside the building.

Despite not getting into the building, the whole episode played out so well, and I knew that we were going to be full-out babyfaces now. This was the coolest thing ever. How could people not like us after this, because the war between the companies was very personal even from a fan's standpoint. Even though fans for the most part watched both shows, they knew there was an intense rivalry. For our fans, even if they thought DX were A-holes, we were now *their* A-holes, and we were a hell of a lot of fun.

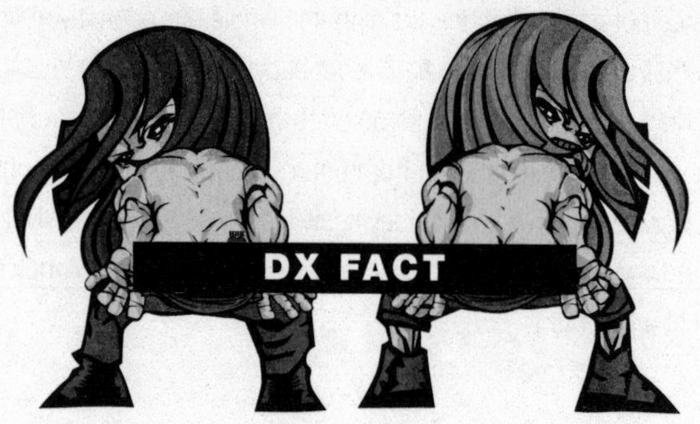

On April 6, 1917, the United States of America declared war on Germany and officially entered World War I. It was eighty-one years later to the day that DX declared war on WCW and invaded their show at the Norfolk Scope.

THE SECOND FRONT

BILLY GUNN

"Just tell Ted [Turner] that D-Generation X is here. I'm sure he'll just send us right up. We're good friends; he really likes us."

HUNTER: Our shock-and-awe offensive in Norfolk produced great dividends. If Stone Cold Steve Austin was number one, then DX was now a solid one-A. Still, the war with WCW had not been won. Like any good army, we pressed our advantage by opening up a second front.

Once we had the great success in Norfolk, we knew we had to keep going with the DX war against WCW. So we put together a list of things we could do. Among the ideas we came up with were going to their training facility, their offices, and the CNN tower.

We decided to go and make fun of their offices first. They were located in some dinky little strip mall outside of Atlanta. We went ahead of time and made a donation to the town's policemen's benevolent association to get on the cops' good side, just in case we needed them. We talked to the chief of police and told him what we were planning to do. So the police were completely on board with us.

We dressed up in our fatigues, enlisted Colonel Woody to drive us around in the jeep with the cannon, and did a bit for the cameras mocking the location of the offices. When the folks at WCW saw us there, they called the police and said they were under attack by a paramilitary organization.

The cops came from everywhere. At first it was a little unnerving seeing all the cops. We thought maybe we were going to jail for trespassing. When they saw us and realized that we had already told them what we were doing, they became more pissed at WCW than at us. I mean, come on, DX is a paramilitary organization? We were just a bunch of jerk-offs having fun.

After that incident, we decided to head down to the CNN tower in Atlanta. We didn't know what was going to happen, and as soon as we arrived we realized that the people at the WCW office had called down and said we might be coming. Security was waiting for us.

We argued with security about going into the building, and just about as they were going to throw us out for good, I saw a guy I knew named Dick Cheatem. I met him when I worked for WCW. He worked at Turner and was a big wrestling fan. I used to talk to him a lot. Most of the guys ignored him because no one knew who he was. Even though I was a nobody at the time, I could see he was a fan and I would go over and talk to him.

So just as we were about to get thrown out for good, I saw Dick coming in. He recognized me and started yelling.

"DX! DX! I love you guys!" He started putting us over in front of everyone and gave us passes to get into the building. It took maybe half an hour until someone upstairs found out what was going on and overrode Dick to get us thrown out.

We were actually going to take the tour of the facility. We would have, but the next tour didn't start before they caught on to us. We didn't make a stink this time because we had this great footage of Turner executives doing the crotch chop and putting us over. It was really entertaining and a bit surreal for us, because here's this executive from Turner letting us walk around and screw off in the CNN center with video cameras.

By this time we were really getting under WCW's skin. We had other stuff we had planned to do. There was a woman who worked in the head office of WCW, and she was tired of working there and was going to come and work for us. WCW ended up doubling her salary so she ended up staying, but in that time period when she was going to leave, she gave us Bischoff's flight itineraries for a couple of weeks out. We were going to ambush-interview him at an airstrip.

As long as we did it under the guise of journalism and asked him questions, then he couldn't do anything to us. A news crew can ask anyone questions in public and there's really nothing you can do about it. So as long as we did it as reporters we would have been perfectly within our rights to do so.

In the end, we decided not to do it though. We had gotten the reaction we wanted by then from a fan standpoint and felt that there really wasn't that much to gain by doing more. We thought the WCW program had run its course. It was really funny, but now we needed to make money by fighting someone within WWE.

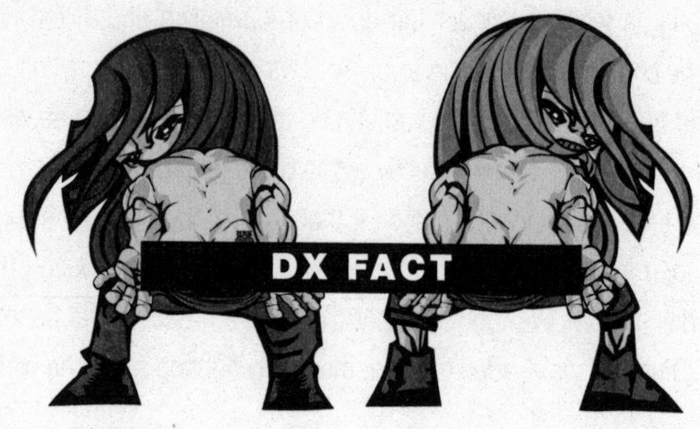

There is plenty of DX merchandise available at WWEShop.com.

DX

COMRADES IN ARMS

"Ladies and gentlemen, boys and girls, children of all ages. D-Generation X proudly presents the badass Billy Gunn, the Road Dogg, Jesse James, the New Age Outlaws!"

HUNTER: When Shawn left after *WrestleMania XIV*, there was a big void for me. My best friend was no longer there. But on the other hand, there was also a huge burden off of me. Shawn was pretty messed up at the time. Sometimes it was a struggle to get him to the shows. There were times when he didn't want to do anything, and there were times when he bitched a lot.

The weeks leading up to *WrestleMania XIV* were the most stressed out I've ever been. There was a good chance Shawn wasn't even going to show up. He was just so angry. Every day he would find some little thing that made him so furious that he was ready to leave. He made outrageous demands on everyone. He tried to be the biggest jerk, and because of our friendship, it was my responsibility to make sure he did what he should do. So when he left, there was a part of me that was relieved because he had been so out of control.

With Dogg, Billy, Kid, and Chyna, we just had fun. We all got along. With Shawn and me, it was different. We were by ourselves. It went very quickly from anger and heat and people wanting to kill us, to people loving us in the new incarnation of DX. With Shawn we had a friendship and all we had was each other, and we formed a close bond.

With the four of us now, it was just like being in college or high school with a bunch of other jack-offs—together with Chyna, who played at being the straight person in the group. We would go out and do the dumbest things we could think of. Whatever we thought was funny, we would do. Sometimes it was funny and sometimes it really sucked. Sometimes it was so bad it was funny. But it was just off-the-cuff stuff. Most of it was us just trying to make each other laugh.

We were doing everything on the fly, and it would work because we had a similar sense of humor. Road Dogg might be the funniest guy on the planet. The Armstrongs are all funny, and Brian is probably the funniest out of all of them. When Brian and I rode together when we were in DX, all we would do is laugh. My abs would hurt from laughing so much at the end of a four-day run with him.

So we didn't have any trouble getting things started. Billy was much more serious. He can be funny, but he's usually pretty serious. But he laughed at our funny stuff. Kid was kind of slow and would fall behind, but then every now and then he would just say something really funny and we'd all crack up laughing. He was never the instigator of the funny stuff, but he always chimed in, plus he always laughed at everything.

As far as the comedy aspect, it was probably mostly Brian and I. Billy had good ideas but his ideas were like, "What if we did this?" And that's something you could do next week. He wasn't an immediately ha-ha kind of guy. And Chyna is actually pretty funny, but it wasn't her role to be funny. Every now and then she would lean to one of us and say, "You guys should do this," and we'd go do it.

One time we were taping a *Raw* at Madison Square Garden and the show ended up being a couple of minutes short for the two-hour block that would run the next week. So Vince asked us for a favor. He said, "We'll send you to New York City with a camera crew, and do whatever you want. Shoot whatever you want."

So we went to the city with the camera crew and they asked us what we wanted to do. Of course we had no idea, so we just set off and did whatever came to mind. We spent the whole day joking with people and getting girls to show us their boobs, which is ridiculously easy in New York City, by the way. We had gotten to the point where they just told us to be jerk-offs in front of the camera, and that's what we did.

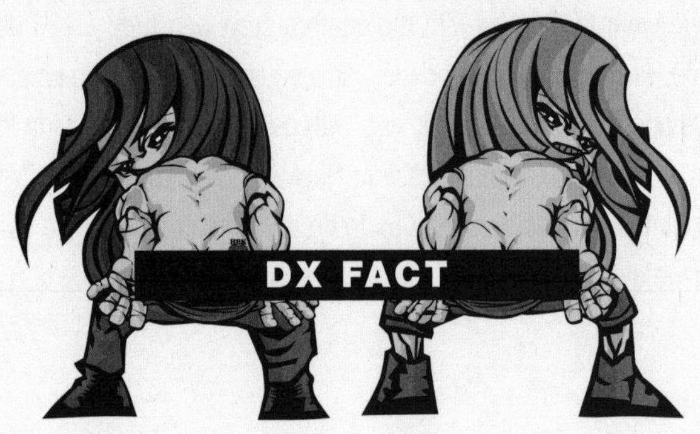

DX has never lost a match on the Asian continent.

DX

RAW
WAR
CAUTION

THE DX NATION

THE CROCK

"You know, The Crock just came from the bathroom, and woooooooohh! You should have smelled what The Rock was cooking!"

B'LO

"I ain't fakin', you should have smelled what The Rock was bakin'."

THE CROCK

"As a matter of fact, when it comes to The Crock and the ladies, and The Crock hits rock bottom, he has no choice but to lay the smackdown on himself."

HUNTER: On July 6, 1998, we pulled off our first parody. In this instance we played the part of The Nation. As usual our actions were not without controversy.

It was fun doing The Nation parody. The creative team

told us to dress up like The Nation and make fun of them so we could turn it into a program. Kid did not want to do it. I remember having to hold his arms out so he could put the sweatshirt on over his fat pad so that he could be Mark Henry. He was like a little child, saying, "I'm not doing this. This is stupid."

He really hated the idea. Then when we got out there and the people started reacting to it, he was really hilarious. When we got to the back he couldn't stop talking about how great it was, and I was like, "Shut up! You didn't even want to do it in the first place."

When we all sat down trying to come up with verbiage and a game plan, I remember Rock was very sensitive about race. He came to me during the day and said he thought it was wrong that we were putting black paint on our faces like it was a minstrel show.

I explained that we weren't making fun of you because you are black, we were just making fun of you. If I didn't go out looking black, if I am ghostly white, then I'm not The Rock, and I just look like an idiot. Mark Henry is really dark. If Kid went out there pasty white like he is naturally, he's not going to look like Mark Henry and the skit won't work. Still, Rock was against it. I think once he saw what we did he was OK with it because he saw that it wasn't about being black. It was about making fun of those characters.

This parody was the kind of thing you could do with ten different people and get ten entirely different kinds of skits. But I think with the gel that we had as a group, we were able to do this kind of work really well. And once the creative team saw what we could do, they felt that they could do just about anything with us.

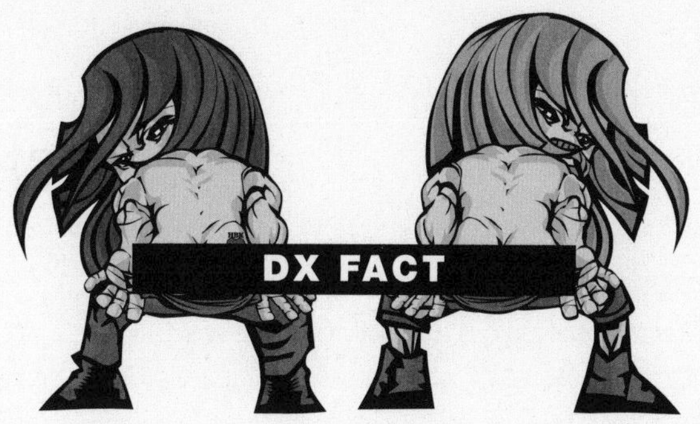

The New Age Outlaws won the tag team title four times while competing.

CHAOS

HUNTER: The summer and fall of 1998 proved to be tumultuous times for D-Generation X. I was moving forward with my singles career, and I won my first Intercontinental title by beating The Rock in a Ladder match at *SummerSlam*. Unfortunately, a knee injury put me on the shelf, and I was stripped of the title shortly thereafter.

Chyna got involved in a rather sordid relationship with Marc Henry (in a story line), who ultimately ended up filing a sexual harassment suit against her. X-Pac traded the European Championship with D'Lo Brown, while the New Age Outlaws lost and won their tag team titles to Kane & Mankind, before losing them to the Corporation's Ken Shamrock & Big Boss Man.

In November, Shawn made a brief return to World Wrestling Federation.

SHAWN: I did?

HUNTER: Hey, welcome back. Remember, you turned on me, joined Vince's Corporation, and became the World Wrestling Federation commissioner.

SHAWN: That's right. The original idea was to play off you burying me after *WrestleMania XIV* and then carry on a lengthy feud. It didn't turn out to be that lengthy, did it?

HUNTER: No, Shawn, it didn't.

After all the invasion angles, we knew that we had to start creating internal story lines that we could make money off of. It started with The Nation parody. I began feuding with The Rock. Chyna had her deal with Marc Henry. X-Pac was fighting with D'Lo Brown, and Billy & Dogg had their battles with other strong tag teams. Even though we all had our own things going on, it was still good for DX because everything was done under the guise of DX.

As far as my career was concerned, my knee was the big issue. I hurt it really bad that fall. I had been having trouble with it for a while—the original problem actually started back when I was with Shawn in DX, and it just kept getting progressively worse.

The doctors originally thought it was just a trauma injury, but what it turned out to be was a loose tendon. As a result I didn't have any stability, and my knee would pop out of its socket. I wanted to put off surgery as long as possible, so what would happen is that I would injure myself, take a little time from rigorous wrestling, and let it heal.

Eventually they would let me wrestle again, but I would invariably reinjure my knee. I went through this cycle several times, and each time my knee would pop out it would get more and more painful.

By the time I got to the Ladder match with Rock at *SummerSlam*, I was having it taped, wrapped, and wore two braces on it. My kneecap was sliding out all the time. My leg was completely unstable, and I couldn't train. It was really affecting me and limiting what I could do in the ring. Finally Dr. Andrews said we were out of options, and I really needed to have surgery to tighten up the tendon. The doctors went in and shrank the tendon down to make it tighter and give me the stability I needed. Of course I couldn't wrestle for a while, so I was stripped of the title. Sometimes when you can't wrestle because of injury, you lose momentum, but I wasn't worried because I was still going to be on the shows.

SHAWN: As for me, the fact is, I just wasn't ready to come back when I did. My back was really killing me. I had put off surgery, and it just wasn't getting any better. I wasn't going to be able to wrestle.

Mentally, I also wasn't ready to come back. I had left in March on a very bitter note and hadn't yet made peace with myself. I was very happy for Hunter and the rest of DX for all the success they were having, but I couldn't enjoy it as much as I should have because of the bitterness that I still carried within myself. Looking back, I realize that until I cleared that up, I wasn't going to be able to work.

The company was great to give me a chance to come back then, but it wasn't going to work. I ended up having back surgery in January 1999, and it would be another two years before I was in the proper shape to come back full time. OK, see you later.

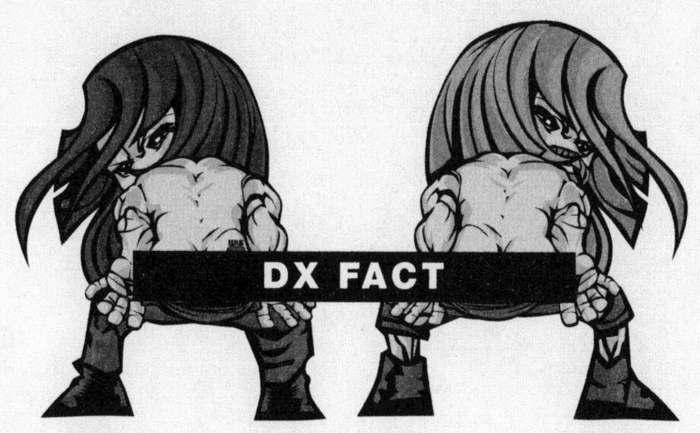

Triple H isn't the only DX member to lead an invasion of WCW. Shawn pulled off an even bigger coup when he swept in and won the heart of a WCW *Nitro* Girl—his wife, Rebecca—in 1999.

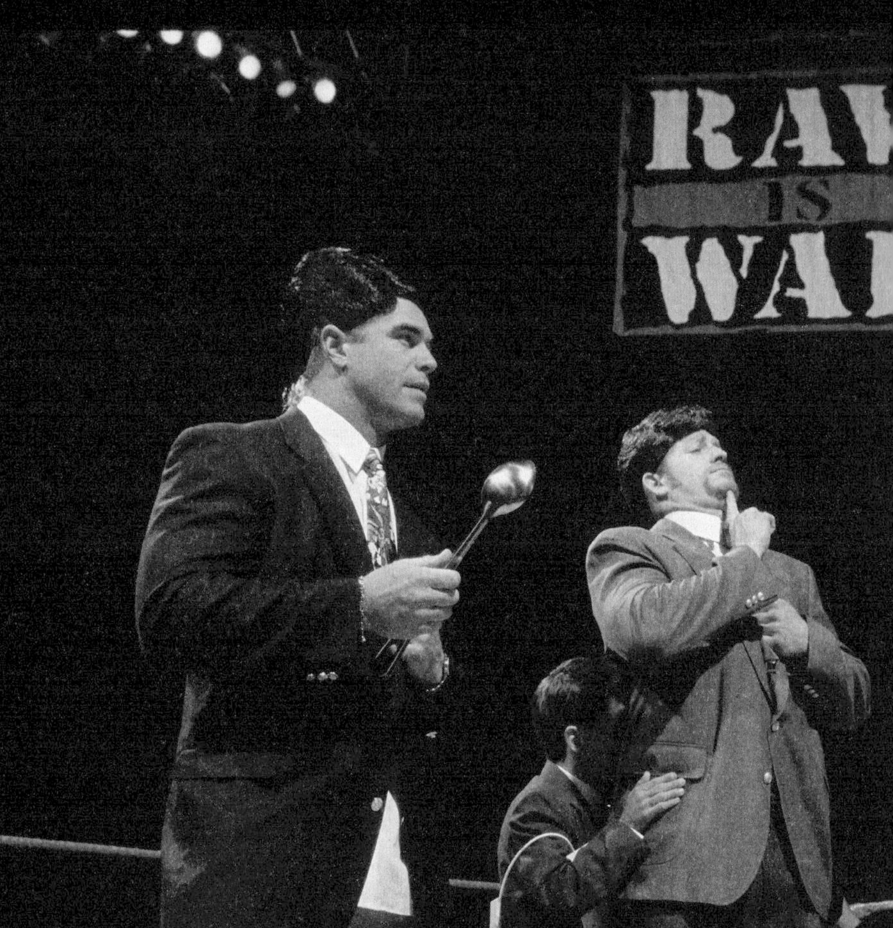
RA
IS
WA

CORPORATION DX

VINCE MCMAHON

"First of all, ladies and gentlemen, let me make one thing perfectly clear, mind you, I am an a**hole . . . Shane, have you got poopies in your diaper? . . . Mr. Brisco, does my a** taste good?"

THE CROCK

"And when The Craaaahhhck is not taking his own coooooorporate head, and sticking it up his own coooooorporate a**, he's got his own two cooooorporate lips buried down deep inside Mr. McMahon's sphincter . . . If you don't get what DX is saying then there's only one thing and The Crock means onnnne thing left to say, and that's, 'We got two words for you . . .' "

HUNTER: In December of 1998, we did an impersonation of the Corporation. By this time the Mr. McMahon character had been firmly established, so there wasn't the same anger as there was when I first went after Vince in 1997. This was pure humor, and one of the hardest parts was not busting out laughing when Road Dogg was speaking or X-Pac was imitating Ken Shamrock.

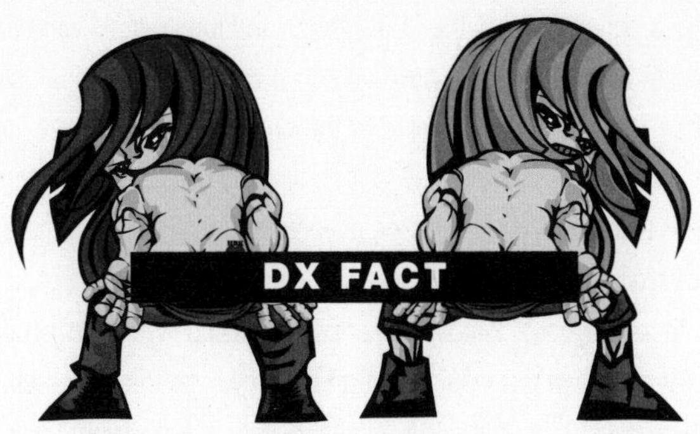

Triple H's DX introductory "Let's get ready to" speech was first done as a goof.

HUNTER: I think I did it in a house show first, just like we used to do when Road Dogg came out with his intro and they would do that and I would do something. One night we were in the ring getting introduced, and Road Dogg went to the ring announcer and told him he was awful and to get out of the ring. And he said let me do some announcing and he did his intro and then I felt that I needed to do something to announce us and so I took the mic and did the Buffer thing. It all happened in like five seconds, no preplanning, and I just decided to say "Let's get ready to suck it" instead of "Let's get ready to rumble." I'm sure it wasn't very good the first time I said it, but I worked on it and it took off. Funny story is, later I heard it caused big heat with Buffer. He actually contemplated suing us. I heard he was very angry about it.

It's like if you do stuff and it makes people laugh, that's kind of how our business works. You'll do something you didn't intend to do, but it gets a hell of a reaction, and if you are in tune with that you'll pick that up and do it again.

It's like Rock's People's Elbow. He was doing that to make us laugh during house shows. He did that a couple of times and someone dared him to do it on TV, and it got a hell of a reaction and the next thing you know he's doing it all the time.

Same thing with us and the Buffer thing, and then people were able to participate and get into it. Like right now we do a two- or three-minute joke routine, but back then I would joke on people in the crowd and it was just funny at the time. Everyone else in the crowd loved it as long as you weren't joking on them. Now people will boo a lot if you pick on anyone, but at that time if there was a fat guy in the crowd and we got on them, it was over.

And then the boob thing just kept progressing. We'd do a house show where a semi-attractive girl would do it and then we go to some really hot ones and say oh you have to do it and they would. It just kind of caught on.

I started getting the feeling that people like watching us wrestle but we were also like the rock stars who say this group over here is going to sing this line and this group will sing this line. People just loved the interaction, and it was kind of like being a rock star and controlling the crowd.

We joked sometimes that we should just go out and do that stuff and say thank you very much—not even wrestle—and go in the back because everything else was anticlimactic. We were having so much fun we could take any premise and make it funny.

DX

ON FIRE

HUNTER: By the beginning of 1999, we had a lot of crazy things going on, including a lot of dissension within DX. Not long after the Corporation parody, the New Age Outlaws left DX and joined the once hated Corporation. Chyna, too, turned on the D-Generate Nation, leaving me and X-Pac as the sole surviving members of DX.

While X-Pac focused his energy on battling Shane McMahon for the European Championship, I became embroiled in a heated rivalry with Kane and Chyna. They planned several twists and turns to keep the story interesting, but not everything went according to plan.

As part of my program with Kane and Chyna, the creative team set up a scene where Kane would hit her with a fireball. Then I would come back a week later with this massive flamethrower and light Kane on fire.

Chyna didn't want to do it. She was worried that she would get hit in the face or her hair would burn. She didn't think it was safe. I told her not to worry, that it's safe, and that we do this all the time in the business.

The way it worked was that there was this little gun that Kane held in his hand. The gun had a little piece of wadded-up fire paper. The gun was spring-loaded, so that Kane pulled the trigger, the trigger would spark, light the paper on fire, and shoot it out toward Chyna. It's just a quick flash, but it looks like this gigantic flame. And it was supposed to be completely burned out by the time it got to Chyna. I kept telling her not to worry: "By the time it gets to you, it's burned out."

We spent all day talking her into doing the scene and even rehearsed it several times. It worked perfectly every time.

We get there live, and we are in the ring and Kane shoots off the paper. This time it traveled a little farther than it did in practice. It ended up hitting her right above the eye and exploding into flames right next to her face. Exactly what we said wouldn't happen *did* happen.

She was so pissed off. It burned part of her eyebrow and burned off her eyelashes. I remember thinking, "What can I say?" I apologized, but let's just say I wasn't forgiven right away.

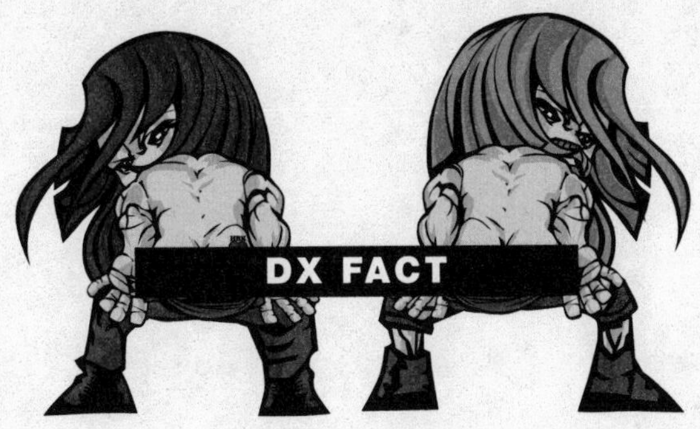

Shortly after *WrestleMania XV*, X-Pac started teaming up with Kane in tag team combinations. The team fared quite well, winning multiple championships. Perhaps the highlight of their run came shortly after Kane learned to speak. One of the first things he said, compliments of X-Pac, was "Suck it!"

THE END?

HUNTER: A little before *WrestleMania XV*, Vince asked me what I wanted to do next in my career. I thought about how successful DX was, but I didn't get into the business to sell T-shirts or make people laugh. I got into the business to be a big star in my own right. My goal was to be a successful singles heel. That's what I felt I was really good at. Even though I enjoyed all the comedy things we were doing, I liked all the heat that Shawn and I created and I enjoyed being a dick and a heel.

So I had a difficult decision to make. Should I stay as a comedy guy in DX or move on to something else on my own? I decided to move on with my singles career, and to do that, I needed to change my character.

I saw a big void in the business for a working heel. Austin was a huge babyface, and Rock was going to be one; even Undertaker, when he was working as a heel, still had a following and was more of a monster heel than a working heel in the manner of Ric Flair in his heyday. I saw that Austin and The Rock needed someone to go up against, because as a babyface, you are only as good as the heel and vice versa. They needed someone to be Darth Vader to their Luke Skywalker, otherwise it wasn't going to work. I wanted to fill that void. So the opportunity was prime.

When the creative team went to the rest of DX and told them that I was going to turn and leave, they were angry. But I was like, "What do you want me to do?"

So the plan was set in motion where Chyna would walk out on us and join the Corporation. Then she would team up with Kane, who I would wrestle at *WrestleMania XV*. At *WrestleMania* she would turn on Kane, and it would look like we were reuniting and all would be well with DX. That only lasted a short time, though, as I screwed over X-Pac in his match against Shane. That was the moment of my heel turn and my tenure in DX . . . for now.

INTO THE WILDERNESS AND ON TO THE PROMISED LAND

HUNTER: The night after *WrestleMania XV*, X-Pac officially declared that DX would go on without me, and that he and the New Age Outlaws would write a new chapter in DX history. Unfortunately, it wasn't a very interesting chapter.

We had gotten to the point where we had done so much so fast that we were running out of steam. Billy Gunn soon turned solo, then he and I briefly teamed up to fight X-Pac and Road Dogg for the rights to the DX name. X-Pac and Road Dogg's victory provided the rationale for me to fully embark on a singles career and realize one of my dreams.

After *WrestleMania XV* I started to get over as a heel, and it was pitched that I would win the World Wrestling Federation Championship title from Steve Austin. I was going to be the first guy who beat Austin clean in the middle of the ring. It was going to happen at *SummerSlam* and Jesse Ventura was going to be the special guest referee.

A few weeks before the match, Steve hurt his knee. He wasn't going to be able to perform up to his usual standards, so he came up with the idea to put Mick Foley in the match and turn it into a Triple Threat match. With Mick there, Steve wouldn't have to do as much and it would be easier on his knee.

Nothing was set in stone until the *Raw* show right before the Pay-Per-View.

Vince came up to me and said that because Steve's knee was messed up, they were going to put just Foley in the match and have Mick beat Austin. The following night, I would beat Mick and win the title. Vince believed that it would be better if I won the title in a one-on-one match on live TV. I didn't agree completely, but I was so thrilled to become champion I wasn't going to make a big deal out of it.

I was really happy to be the top heel. At the time, it was still arguable whether I was the guy for that role. The business was different back then. Today, someone may win the title to help get them over, but back then it was a really big deal to win the title. It was like Vince saying, "I trust you to be the face of the entire company."

Vince called me into his office and gave me the big speech of how I had earned this and how he had trust in me. It was everything I dreamed of when I got into this business. At the time, just being thought of in that role was big enough for me. The other thing that made me feel really good was that Vince didn't see me as a brief champion. He wanted me to hold the title for a long time. We might switch it briefly for a bit, but the plan was to build me as a heel that he could put some heat on for a while. You can look at the history of this company, and I'm one of the very few heels who's had a long title run. This was the beginning of it, so it was really gratifying.

Being part of DX helped get me to this position. I'd like to think that everything in my career happened for a reason, and without a doubt what came before helped me get to and handle being the champion. If they had come to me six months earlier and told me they wanted to put the title on me, I wouldn't have known what to do with it. Now I felt like I knew what to do. Of course, looking back on it now, I wish I knew a little more than I did when I won it, but you are always learning in this business, so that's pretty normal.

At that time, it just felt right. The babyfaces wanted to work with me. I believed my skills in the ring were good enough, I felt my mic skills were good enough. I had to revamp the character and change a lot of stuff, but I knew where I wanted to go and I was ready for it.

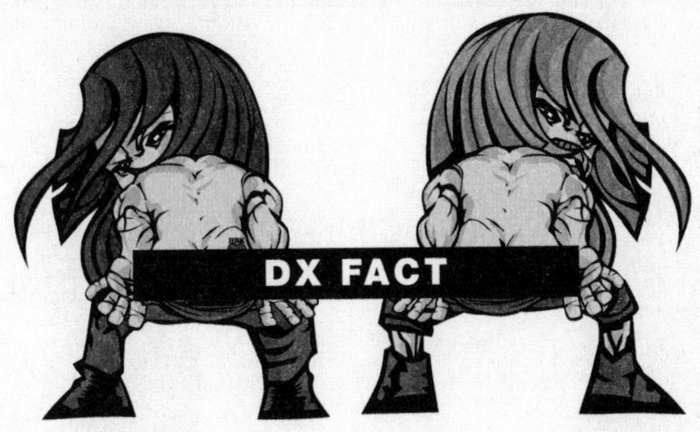

Shawn and Hunter have seventeen world championships between the two of them—one more than their hero Ric Flair, who has sixteen.

The cameraman wanted to film the consummation of the marriage, but that didn't happen.

LOVE DX STYLE

HUNTER: One month after I won the World Wrestling Federation Championship, Road Dogg & Billy Gunn reunited and won the Tag Team Championship by defeating The Rock & Mankind. One month later, DX officially reunited when X-Pac and I helped the New Age Outlaws defeat The Rock & Stone Cold Steve Austin in a Tag Team match.

DX was back and on top of the world. We were far from resting on our laurels though . . .

Vince Russo, who was our lead writer at the time, had this concept for a story where Vince's daughter would marry one of the boys. He had worked it to the point where Stephanie had fallen in love with Test and they had planned a wedding. The only thing was, he had no idea where he was going to go with it after the wedding. He didn't know what the final result would be.

We were two weeks out from the wedding and neither Russo nor anyone else had come up with a good story for what would happen after the wedding. Russo then bolted for WCW and we were really under the gun. That's why we ran the scene where Stephanie got hit in the head with a garbage can, got amnesia, and didn't remember who Test was. That was done purely to buy time for us so that we could figure out what to do.

I was in the middle of feuding with Vince, and I believe it was actually Chyna who said, "You know, the worst guy in the world that she could marry is you. Could you imagine that?"

Once Chyna said that, it made me start thinking how much heat Vince and I would have if that happened. I didn't even really know Stephanie at the time. I would say hello to her when I saw her, but we weren't friends or anything.

So I saw Vince, and I asked him if he knew where he was going with the whole Stephanie wedding. He told me that they hadn't decided on anything.

I then proposed the idea that they have this bachelorette party for Stephanie while Test has his bachelor party. Somehow at the bachelorette party, viewers see I pay a guy to Mickey her drink, and I take her, nearly unconscious, to an all-night wedding chapel. She ends up getting married to me the night before her wedding to Test. But none of this airs until the wedding. So just when Test and Stephanie are about to exchange their vows, I come out and say she can't get married to Test because she is married to me. At this point, I show the footage from the night before. Stephanie is devastated because she was unconscious from the Mickey, and Vince, of course, is beyond furious with me. Vince told me he loved the idea, and a few days later we were in Vegas shooting it.

The second part to the story is that we had to figure out how I could get a shot at the title because Vince had banned me from ever getting one. My pitch to him was that he and I have a match, and if I win I get a shot at the title. If he wins I annul the marriage.

Well, the next time on TV, Stephanie went out to explain herself. She was trying to garner sympathy, but the fans had a hard time liking her anyway, being the billionaire princess and all. She went out to try and explain herself, and she was crying, but our hardcore fans started to really get on her, chanting, "Whore!" and "Slut!"

I remember sitting there and Vince tapping me and saying we were going to run with this. Once this happened Vince's wheels started turning, and he said,

"What if she turns on me? And you two hook up and I can't take it anymore and just disappear? When I'm gone, Stephanie takes over the show." This story was now really taking on a life of its own.

At *Armageddon,* I'm fighting Vince for the title shot or annulment, and Vince is about to hit me with a sledgehammer. Stephanie then comes into the ring and says to Vince, "Let me hit this dirtbag." She takes the sledgehammer and looks like she is going to hit me, but she just can't do it. When she turns around to walk away, I grab the hammer and whack Vince and beat him. Then she comes and celebrates with me. It was a huge double swerve and the place was going nuts. It turned out great, considering we had no idea where we were going just two weeks before the wedding, but sometimes that's how it goes in this business.

HHH
HEAD

FIGHTING THE MAN

HUNTER: Vince and I had plenty of verbal confrontations dating all the way back to the genesis of DX in 1997. *Armageddon*, however, was the first time we officially squared off in the ring. It's one thing to get in a verbal confrontation with the Chairman. It's quite another to get physical with him.

There are both good and bad things when it comes to working with Vince. He's a great performer. He has a lot of intensity and a great sense of humor too. I've worked with him from both sides, where I've been a heel and he's been a babyface, and where I've been a babyface and he's been a heel. He's a lot of fun to be with out there.

From a match standpoint he's a lot of fun because he's willing to do anything. The bad part is, he's not real good. He has limited mobility, he's beat up physically, and you really have to work around him. During the Street Fight match that he and I had at *Armageddon* where Stephanie turned on him, we did a bump where we fell about thirty feet from a scaffolding.

Earlier in the day we decided to practice it. I did it twice with Shane so Vince could see it, and then I went up on the scaffolding with Vince to go through it. We were supposed to fall off it at the same time, but Vince stutter-stepped falling off the platform. I ended up a second ahead of him, falling off the platform, and he faded to the side instead of falling straight down. So when he landed, he landed right on my left leg and just about broke it. My leg felt like it was bent in half backward. It was painful as hell.

This was just a few hours before the Pay-Per-View. I was rolling around in agony, thinking I had a broken leg, and he's all worried and feeling terrible. I went to the training room, got iced up, took some anti-inflammatories, and took a shot of Toradol. I was doing everything to get it not to swell so that I could work.

We taped my leg up so tight it was as if it were in a cast, and I was able to do the match. It's just funny working with him—a hazard of the job, I guess.

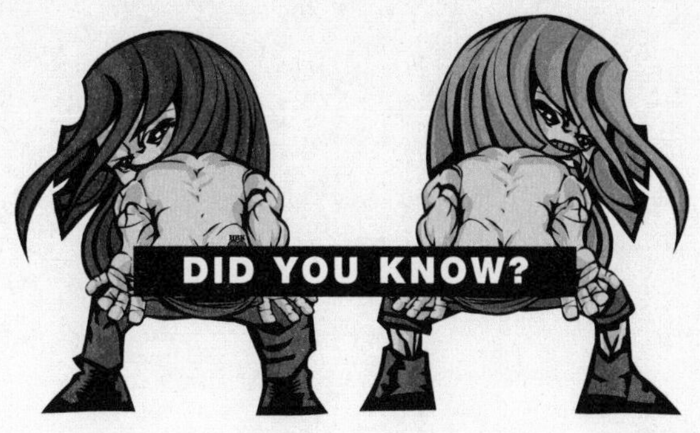

In order to agitate Vince before the match at *Armageddon*, DX set Vince's office on fire. They started it by feeding Mr. Ass beans and igniting a lighter under his derrière.

THE DX EXPRESS

HUNTER: At *WrestleMania XVI*, I retained the World Wrestling Federation Championship in a Fatal Four Way match and turned heel by teaming up with Vince. Not too long afterward, DX celebrated by buying a new vehicle to ride in from show to show: the DX Express luxury bus.

I think the whole point of getting the bus was so that Steve Austin could blow it up. I really don't recall there being anything else to getting the bus. The story was that Steve was coming back to the company and no one knew whether he was going to side with me or Rock at our match at *Backlash*. I guess blowing up our bus was a way of showing everyone that he wasn't going to be siding with me.

Austin blowing up the bus turned out to be unintentionally hilarious. I'm just glad that we were in the ring when it happened rather than being in the bus.

First off, earlier in the day, we were sitting in the bus and Road Dogg was smoking a cigarette. Someone came running up to us and said, "Guys, you have to get out of there, this thing is rigged with explosives and could blow up!"

No one had told us that. When they showed us underneath that all the storage bays were filled with explosives, we were like, "Holy crap! We could have blown ourselves to bits!"

During the show, the plan was that when we were in the ring, Steve was going to hit the bus with a wrecking ball and it was going to explode. I don't know how they worked the whole thing out from Steve's perspective, but Steve almost killed himself with the wrecking ball. He started to swing it, and it got out of control and almost hit him in the cab. We thought he was done for.

He finally got the wrecking ball under control and he managed to hit the bus and nothing happened. It literally went "dink." We are all in the ring, and the live crowd started laughing. Meanwhile, Steve's in the back there trying to fix the situation, and there are probably five to eight minutes of him tapping it the first time and then him nailing it and it blowing up.

I mean, it's funny. We're trying not to laugh at our top babyface. The crowd is laughing, Steve's pissed, and everyone can really see he's pissed. Vince tried to buy some time by making a joke about it, and then he said, "Triple H is going to tell you what's up."

I had nothing to say to make the save, so I just passed the microphone to Road Dogg, who had nothing to say, and he passed the mic on, and so it went. It was just brutal. And when Steve was finally able to hit the bus, he dropped the wrecking ball and it came down like a half mile an hour and the bus explodes. It was completely ridiculous live.

We got out of the ring, and we were thinking this is going to be the most embarrassing thing in the world. We didn't think TV could save it. The people in the arena were just shitting on it. Poor Steve wanted to crawl up his own ass.

Fortunately it was a *SmackDown!* taping, and the TV folks had time to make it look great. They edited out the delay and sped up the drop of the wrecking ball. They made it look so good that they used it as the opener of *Raw* for years. But in reality it was a nightmare.

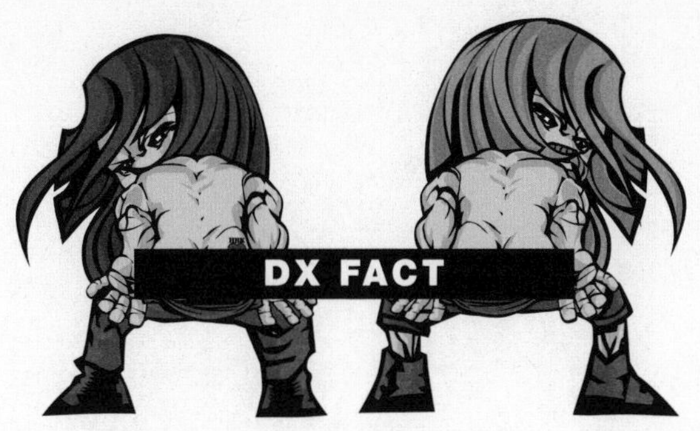

It cost WWE more than $70,000 to blow up the DX Express.

THE SIXTY-MINUTE MAN

HUNTER: Not too long after *WrestleMania XVI*, DX once again faded from center stage. Stephanie and I formed the McMahon-Helmsley Regime and took control of WWE. Our antics angered a lot of fans and Superstars, but perhaps the most significant moment of the McMahon-Helmsley Regime took place in the ring at *Judgment Day*. For on that day, The Rock and I went where only two others had gone before.

The Iron Man match with Rock was a very big deal for me because at that point in time it was only the second Iron Man match in modern WWE history. A lot of people talk about really brutal matches, like Hell in a Cell and Elimination Chamber, but to me, the test of what we do from a performance standpoint is the Iron Man match.

In today's world, where people don't have the patience to watch stuff for more than five minutes and most of the matches they see on our show are eight minutes or less, it's a real challenge to keep them interested in a match for an hour. When you tell most guys on our roster that they have a twenty-minute match, they crap their pants. I could count the guys on one hand here who could go sixty minutes today.

I am proud of it for both myself and Rock. It's not like I did it alone. There was a weird chemistry between me and Rock. We came up at the same time and there was always a rivalry between us. I think the competition led us to excel in a lot of ways. I believe we brought out the best in each other. I don't want to say we didn't get along, but we weren't close friends by any means outside of the ring. Still, when we got in the ring together, we had good chemistry. I had that with Austin too. There was that extra spark there.

Most people ask me how tiring the Iron Man match was, but to tell the truth, I didn't find it to be that physically draining. As a matter of fact, I've never had a match where I felt completely gassed wind-wise, where I couldn't breathe or move. I remember after the match I was so pumped up, I was thinking I could go do another one. It was more tiring mentally. We were constantly thinking and improvising to keep it interesting, and that does become taxing. But I looked at it like a challenge, and I thought Rock and myself rose to the occasion.

It was a ton of fun. For us it's the ultimate challenge. The day you stop thriving on that pressure to perform you shouldn't be here. I love Undertaker and Shawn, but when Shawn goes out there and tears it up, I think to myself that I have to up my game. That's my goal and that's what everyone's goal should be: to try and have the match that steals the show when you can.

Rock was always one of my toughest opponents, but we brought out the best in each other.

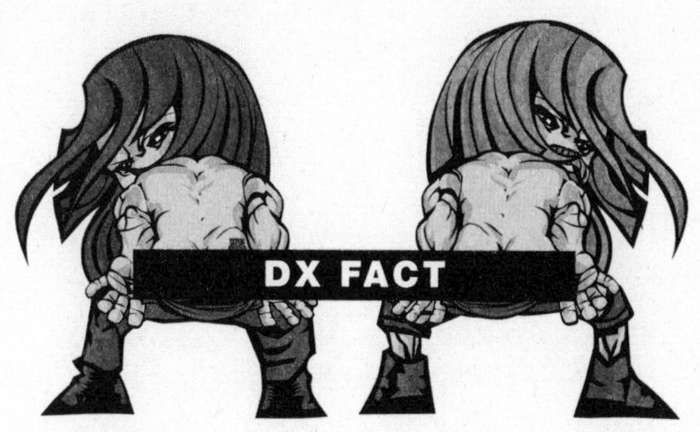

SHAWN: My Iron Man match against Bret Hart at *WrestleMania XII* lasted sixty-two minutes. So while Hunter and Rock's Iron Man match was very impressive, it wasn't quite as impressive as my Iron Man match.

HUNTER: Those shorts you were wearing while refereeing our Iron Man match were pretty impressive too.

ACT THREE

BREAK HIM DOWN

GENERATION

THE PLAYERS

D-GENERATION X

Shawn Michaels: a.k.a. Showstopper; the Icon; Main Event; Heartbreak Kid; HBK. The four-time World Champion and no longer resident bad boy. As a matter of fact, he's so not cool, he's cool.

Triple H: a.k.a. Hunter Hearst-Helmsley; Hunter; The Game; the Cerebral Assassin; King of Kings. Thirteen-time World Champion. Still known for his quick wit, ring psychology, and exceptionally large genitalia.

OTHER KEY PLAYERS

Batman: a.k.a. the Caped Crusader. A superhero who lives in Gotham and, according to Shawn Michaels, bears a not-so-strange resemblance to Triple H.

Vince McMahon: a.k.a. Mr. McMahon; the Chairman; the Genetic Jackhammer. WWE chairman of the board, who remains obsessed with running DX out of WWE and just can't seem to get the job done.

Shane McMahon: a.k.a. Shane O Mac; Here Comes the Money. The Chairman's son, whose daring exploits in the ring are only surpassed by his obsession with dancing.

Stephanie McMahon: a.k.a. the Billionaire Princess. The Chairman's daughter, who bares a striking resemblance to Triple H's wife in real life.

Jonathan Coachman: a.k.a. Coach; The Coach. The Chairman's executive assistant, whose record of incompetence and failure is unmatched in company history.

Big Dick Johnson: WWE creative team member who likes to oil his body up and dance in a thong.

The Spirit Squad: A group of peppy cheerleaders who, for some unknown reason, Mr. McMahon believes should instill fear in DX.

Big Show: a.k.a. the World's Largest Athlete with the world's largest . . .

Eric Bischoff: The failed former head of WCW, who still believes he's the smartest man in the business and has developed a strange aversion to sardines.

Edge: Triple H impersonator who brings out the serious side of DX.

Randy Orton: Shawn Michaels impersonator who's a lot taller than Shawn.

Hornswoggle: A leprechaun.

Great Khali: An Indian giant.

Boogeyman: He eats worms.

WELCOME BACK

SHAWN: Hunter, how've you been? That's some good stuff you guys did, and you certainly took good care of DX while I was gone, but I must say, it's good to be back.

HUNTER: Thanks, Shawn, and welcome back. You know, I've been talking a lot and kind of need to go to the men's room, if you know what I mean. Why don't you catch everyone up with what was going on with you while you were away.

SHAWN: You're not going to create another masterpiece, are you?

HUNTER: You'll never know, Shawn. I'll see you in a few.

SHAWN: So, as you all know, I left WWE after *WrestleMania XIV*. I was bitter, my back was destroyed, and I thought my career was over. I went home to Texas to try and get my life back in order and figure out what I would be doing for the rest of my life. It wasn't easy. Even with rest, my back wasn't getting any better, and since I'd basically been wrestling my whole adult life, I really had no focus and direction in terms of moving my life forward.

There were a few times when I came back briefly to WWE. Like the time I came back as commissioner, but I really wasn't ready to. I was still too angry and hadn't made peace with myself—or the business, for that matter—and my back was really killing me.

In January of 1999, I finally decided to have surgery on my back. Within a few weeks, I could get around all right, and things started to get better for me.

It was also around this time that I met my future wife, and the love of my life, Rebecca. She helped me turn my life around, and by the time 2002 rolled around, I was not only married, a father, and a Christian, but I was ready to come back to WWE.

It was only going to be a one-shot deal in a match against Hunter. Even though my back was feeling better, I hadn't taken any bumps in the ring and had no idea how I might hold up under the rigors of a match. As you might know, I tend to get beat up a lot when I wrestle, so my back had to be able to take a lot of punishment.

DX, of course, figured in my comeback. A couple of weeks before *SummerSlam,* I came back to *Raw*. Hunter handed me a DX T-shirt and said he had "an idea." Later that night we came out to our music, went to the ring, and did our DX chops. It was then that Hunter attacked and pedigreed me, setting up our match at *SummerSlam*. And as you are well aware, my comeback has lasted slightly longer than one match.

One other thing quickly before Hunter comes back. You see—and I'm not afraid to admit this—I'm not quite as cool as I was back in the original DX days. Hunter doesn't know this. He still looks up to me and thinks I'm the hippest, coolest dude in the world, and I wouldn't want to crush him by letting him know this—Oh, here he comes, time to wrap this up—and so as I was saying, by 2006 it was time for DX to make a comeback.

HUNTER: Hey, Shawn, you got everyone caught up?

SHAWN: Yep, just finished up. How about you? Feeling better?

HUNTER: Much better, much better, thanks. Feeling good. So, where should we pick up the story? Where you join the Mr. McMahon Kiss My Ass Club?

SHAWN: Funny guy, Hunter, funny guy.

HUNTER: Let me just give them a brief rundown of what happened in early 2006 that set the stage for the return of DX.

SHAWN: OK, go ahead.

HUNTER: It all began when Shawn interrupted Vince when Vince was reviewing

Bret Hart's DVD. Shawn told Vince to just get over the Montreal saga. Which, I might add, was a very good suggestion.

SHAWN: Thank you, Hunter.

HUNTER: Vince of course blew his top, threatened to fire Shawn, and in the ensuing weeks tried to get a whole bunch of different Superstars to put Shawn out of action. At *Royal Rumble*, Vince used a bunch of Superstars to distract Shawn and actually eliminated Shawn. A sixty-year-old man eliminating you, that's got to be embarrassing.

SHAWN: I know. It wouldn't have happened to you. You're just so smart, aren't you?

HUNTER: Let me go on. Vince and Shawn continued their feud, and Vince soon sent out the Spirit Squad to do his dirty work. Shawn actually beat them all in a Handicap match, but later that same night, they attacked him. Fortunately for Shawn his old friend Marty Jannetty just happened to be at *Raw* that night—talk about your lucky coincidences—and made the save for Shawn.

The next week, Vince tried to make Marty join his Kiss My Ass Club. This time Shawn came in to save Marty, but—no pun intended—Shane whacked Shawn with a chair and planted Shawn's face and lips on Vince's keester. The following week, Stephanie showed up in the locker room and told Shawn that she was apologizing for Vince's and Shane's actions. When Shawn wasn't looking she Mickeyed Shawn's drink. Later in the show, Vince and Shane performed a beatdown on Shawn. For the next couple of weeks Shawn and the McMahons went back and forth, with Shawn getting the best of them most of the time.

At *WrestleMania 22* Shawn beat Vince and Shane, and that really made Vince lose his mind. He claimed that God had interfered in the match and helped Shawn win. Vince then went on to create his own religion, McMahonism, and continued his vendetta against Shawn.

In May 2006, I got involved when I "accidentally" hit Shane with my sledgehammer instead of Shawn. Of course, that sent Vince off his rocker even more, and both myself and Shawn became the targets of his ire. At this point, there really was only one thing to do.

THE DX RE-FORMATION

SHAWN: Hey, Hunter, you hungry?

HUNTER: Yeah, but we sort of have a story to tell. We're right at the point where we are re-forming DX.

SHAWN: I know, but I'm really hungry. Why don't we run that interview we did about the Re-formation with that German magazine? The one we did with that Martin Luther guy or whatever his name was.

HUNTER: We are big over in Europe.

SHAWN: Mexico, Canada—they love DX in Europe!

HUNTER: Why don't you see if you can find that interview?

SHAWN: I have it right here, see: "*Mein Wienerschnitzel* ist—"

HUNTER: Whoa, whoa, the English version.

SHAWN: Oh yeah, right . . .

DX

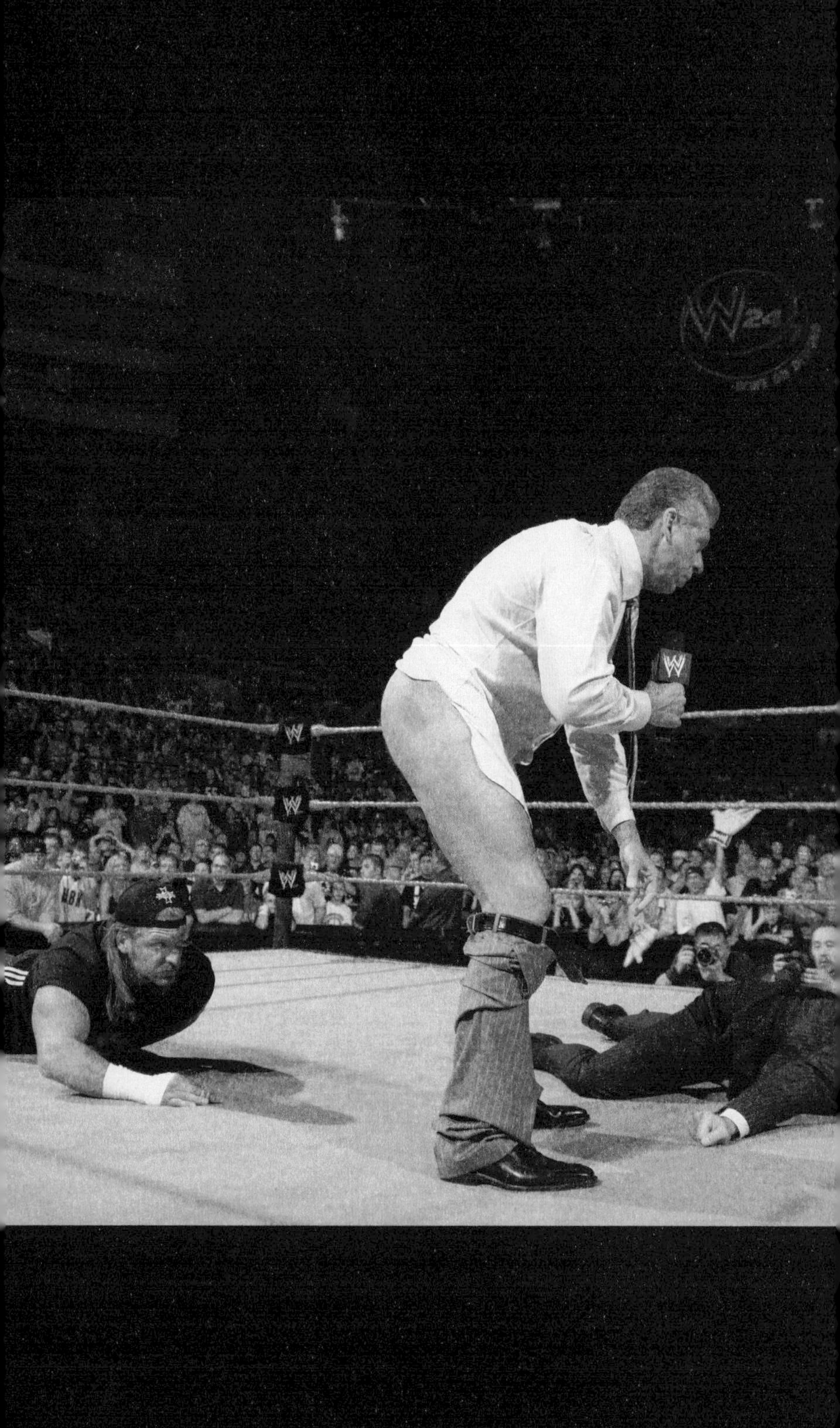

THE DX RE-FORMATION TAKE TWO

VINCE MCMAHON

"There are certain things I would like to discuss with you tonight, and that is what happened to the chairman of the board last week here on *Raw.* It's one thing for me to establish a Kiss My Ass Club, it's quite another for someone who was to join to turn that around and kick me in the guts, wrench arms behind my back, and drive me down to the canvas, thus exposing my derrière in an involuntary basis. There are children who watch this show. I want Triple H to think about that. And something else I want Triple H to think about is what happened to his buddy not too long ago, Shawn Michaels.

"When Shawn Michaels crossed my path, I sicced the Spirit Squad on Mr. Michaels, all five of them. Mr. Michaels is no longer in action. So tonight, Triple H must be taught a lesson, a lesson he will never forget. And yes, once again I will use the Spirit Squad to teach that lesson. However, what will happen tonight,

whatever happened to Shawn Michaels was just too quick. Tonight will be slow. Tonight I will dismember Triple H limb by limb until there is absolutely nothing left, in a Gauntlet match, all five members of the Spirit Squad dismembering Triple H. So tonight, after it's all over, I assure you Triple H will, in fact, be reunited with Shawn Michaels on the highway to hell!"

Dees qvestion ees for Triple H. Shawn Michaels had to join Mr. McMahon's Kees My Ass Club, but you vere able to avoid dis. Ven Shane tried to drug your drink you vere able to switch bottles and outsmart him. How vere you able to do dees?

SHAWN: Let me butt in here. I had to kiss his butt, but of course the whole Mickey-ing the drink thing didn't work on Hunter because he is so much smarter than me and he ends up Pedigreeing Mr. McMahon. I joined his Kiss My Backside Club, he didn't. Let's face it, I'm Robin. Robin gets tied up, Robin always screws up, but thank God there's Batman there to save the day and pull it out of his utility belt.

HUNTER: Let me explain, had this been the earlier version of DX—

SHAWN: No one would have had to Mickey my drink.

HUNTER: C'mon, let me explain. The reason it worked on Shawn now is because he had no tolerance for the Mickey. You see, I'd been preparing myself for this contingency for the last couple of years, slipping little tiny bits of Shawn's old pills into my drinks so that I could build up a resistance to the Mickeys in case the McMahons tried to do something like this. I took a little bit more each time to slowly build my tolerance up. They never affected me but they did build up my tolerance.

But how did you know the McMahons vould try dees?

SHAWN: It was probably because he saw it happen to me a couple of weeks before.

HUNTER: Yes, I watch the show. I saw it happen before. A lot of guys here make the mistake of not watching the actual show.

SHAWN: But if you think about it, the VCR is big. You know, it's like TiVo, but not like TiVo. See, with TiVo you don't have to put anything in the machine, you just tell it what to do.

HUNTER: Yeah, I got TiVo, I have the season pass, so I can see all our shows.

Very interesting. Now, you saw Mr. McMahon in a thong before vou Pedigreed him. Vhat vas going on in your mind?

HUNTER: It's just like every weekend the last four years at our house: Vince running around in a thong.

SHAWN: Well, most guys that age would be running around in boxers. Only Vincent Kennedy McMahon would be in a thong.

HUNTER: I was surprised he didn't have posing trunks on, quite honestly.

Did dees thong disturb vou?

HUNTER: It was not nearly as upsetting as it would have been . . . where it was about to go down the line. You know, we've all seen Vince's butt plenty on the show, so the fact that he had a thong on was not really shocking.

Meester Michaels. Did vou get any satisfaction out of seeing vour buddy get some revenge on the McMahons?

SHAWN: No, none.

HUNTER: The original plan was to have Shawn fall over backward and have to kiss Vince's butt again.

SHAWN: Robin gets no satisfaction, really.

D-GENERATION

This version of the Spirit Squad was about as menacing and threatening as the real thing.

THE REUNION

VINCE MCMAHON

"Two weeks ago on *Raw,* Triple H was to have joined the Mr. McMahon Kiss My Ass Club. I didn't exactly get what I wanted on that night. And then as a result of that, last week, Triple H was to face all five members of the Spirit Squad in a Handicap match. Triple H was to have been dismembered. But thanks to Shawn Michaels, that didn't exactly happen, so I didn't get what I wanted last week either. But this week, I'm going to get exactly what I want.

"You see, I've heard there's supposed to be some kind of DX reunion. There's not going to be any DX reunion tonight. There's simply going to be the destruction of D-Generation X. And you don't believe me? Actions speak louder than words!"

SHAWN: Correct me if I'm wrong, Hunter, but didn't Mr. McMahon sic the Spirit Squad on us the night we made our official reunion?

HUNTER: Yes he did. First of all, there is the genius of Vince McMahon. I know that if I was a billionaire and could get anyone to do my dirty work, it would be—

SHAWN: The Yale Drill Team.

HUNTER: Exactly, the Yale Drill Team, or some type of spirit-loving cheerleaders to pick up my cause. I definitely wasn't scared when I saw the Spirit Squad. Well, not scared for our personal safety. I was worried for the business, though, when I saw them. I thought, "This is the future?" And that scared me.

SHAWN: I think one thing that Vince McMahon—not that we're the biggest, baddest tough guys in the world, the fact is . . .

HUNTER: Shawn can take a beating, though.

SHAWN: As I was saying, Batman, we are fairly credible. There were not a lot of volunteers when Vince asked for people to take on DX. The Spirit Squad were a little naïve and a little young, and obviously full of spirit, but wanting to do anything to make a name for themselves.

HUNTER: I think a lot of the roster looked at all the things that happened to the Spirit Squad—like poop falling on them—and thought they made the right decision not to mess with DX.

SHAWN: Yes, that's sort of my point. There's a little bit of wisdom in the other guys. Let's face it, going up against DX is not always a career enhancer. Again, people will take it out of context because of who we are, the gimmick has always been like that, but the gimmick has always been very powerful. Now, there have been guys who could handle it, like Edge and Randy, but taking on DX takes a guy who knows what he is doing to stand up to DX.

HUNTER: That's definitely true. I think once you've been here for a while and you've been established, you either know how to handle everything that comes with going up against DX or you want nothing to do with it. The Spirit Squad were at a point where, I think if they had been told that we were going to drop three hundred pounds of crap on their heads but they'd get on *Raw*, they would have done it.

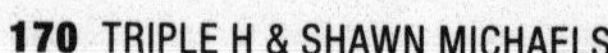

Nothing good comes of messing with DX.

SHAWN: From that perspective, I think I do have a little admiration for them. I think they made the most of it and did everything they could, but it is a daunting task to go up against DX.

Shane O'Mac

STAND BACK!

(The roles of Mr. McMahon and Shane McMahon will be played by Triple H and Shawn Michaels.)

VINCE MCMAHON

"All right, cut my music! Tonight my son, Shane McMahon, and I are going to beat the holy hell out of D-Generation X, but until then I am going to stand here and ramble incoherently for absolutely no reason. What D-Generation X did to me last week was, well, it was embarrassing. It was more embarrassing than when TRIPLE HAITCH Pedigreed me right in the middle of this ring, exposing my doughy white alabaster keester to the world. It's more embarrassing than when SHAAAAAWN MICHAELS beat me within an inch of my life on the grandest stage of them all, *WRESTLE-MAAANIAAAAA.* And quite frankly, it's more embarrassing than . . . than . . . well, than the XFL. You see, D-Generation X last week brought me a rooster, the implication being that I love cocks. Well, I don't. What I like are men, great men who are pioneers, men like my good friend at NBC, Dick Ebersol; men like the vice president of the United States, Dick Cheney; or that great entertainer, that guy who is almost as old as I am, Dick Clark. What I am getting at is that I, VKM, love . . ."

SHANE MCMAHON

"DAD! What are you doing? I'm your son. See, it says so right here in my business card. Dad! I've tried to be supportive of you through this whole thing. Now, mostly because when you die—honestly, I hope it isn't far off—the whole McMahon empire will be mine, mine, mine!"

VINCE MCMAHON

"Son, are you mildly retarded? Shano, you've got it all wrong, kiddo. When I pass, I am not going to leave all my money to you. When I pass, I am going to leave all my money to my beautiful daughter, Stephanie, and whoever that guy is who knocked her up. You know, there is something about that guy . . ."

SHANE MCMAHON

"No way, Dad, no way. You try and leave that money to Stephanie and wham. [Dances.] Dad, this is about DX. At *WrestleMania,* Shawn Michaels took this face and shoved it up your keester . . . I'm getting so excited, look, Dad, I'm dancing, Dad, I'm dancing."

MR. MCMAHON

"You want to play, pal? You want to dance? Well then, you and everybody else had better . . . 'Stand Back'!"

JIM ROSS

"How humiliated, on his own broadcast, can Mr. McMahon and his son, Shane, be?"

SHAWN: People ask us how we felt we did imitating the McMahons, and I have to say that Hunter did an exceptional job. He nailed the walk, and what can you say about when "Stand Back" came on? I think Hunter set new standards in his imitation of Vince dancing. I blew up myself as long as it was going. But I have to give him a solid eight, eight and a half, out of ten.

HUNTER: For Shawn, I will go a ten. Vince is a gimme, he is a straight gimmick. All I had to do was pull my pants up to my armpits and swing my arms a lot. And his voice—well, after hearing him yell at us all these years, it's very easy. Shane is a little bit different and more difficult to do. He's less of an over-the-top character. Although after Shawn's performance he may not be so now. The hardest thing for me during the entire skit was me not laughing at him doing Shane dancing around. I just kept trying to look away from Shawn to keep from laughing.

SHAWN: Thank you, Hunter, but I can't take all the credit. Like everything else, you try and get everyone's opinion. The great thing around here is that there are enough people who watch our shows closely enough that they can give you little details and break down the moves and facial stuff. One thing that DX does is that once you get on to something, you beat that son of a gun and you beat it and beat it.

HUNTER: Even if it's not funny, you just keep beating it until it is funny.

SHAWN: Exactly. If you do things so many times, eventually the people become delirious and it's actually pretty funny. That was the theory behind the Shane dancing.

HUNTER: And quite honestly, a lot of the things we do we think are quite funny. A lot of times we'll bounce stuff off each other and be like, "I think that's really funny, but is anyone else going to think it's funny?"

SHAWN: That goes back to the genesis of DX; we would do stuff that we thought was funny but no else did.

HUNTER: But we thought it was funny, and that's all that mattered. That's something that still works for us today.

SHAWN: Right. And there were times I could remember that there were only a few of us who thought something was funny: me, Hunter, John Cena, and one of our writers, Ed. But if the four of us laughed, then it was gold and we were going with it.

HUNTER: The unfortunate thing for Shawn was that "Stand Back" started and it just kept going and going. That was one of the few times someone got one over on us, because it was just supposed to run for a few seconds, but someone decided to play the whole song.

SHAWN: And it was live TV. That was Vince in the back saying, "OK, you guys want to play games, let's play games."

HUNTER: But Shawn had been dancing and doing Shane's spastic stuff for the entire duration of the promo, and then on top of that "Stand Back" came on. I was just standing around the whole time before "Stand Back" came on, and I was blown sky high from having to dance through the song, I know he had to be dying. He just kept dancing by me, saying, "This is a rib, this is a rib."

As everyone could probably tell, I had no idea what I was doing. I can't dance. At that point I was thinking Vince's dancing in the video is funny, but when the music hits, I'm just going to bust loose and do the craziest dance moves I could do. I don't know how you would classify it other than awful, which was pretty much the point. And since I can't dance I really didn't have to put that much effort into making it ridiculous. It was rotten enough to be funny. Which is why I don't dance, because that's probably how I would.

SHAWN: I think our hair looked pretty good too, don't you?

HUNTER: That's a credit to Jan, our makeup lady. It's about creating something outrageous, and if you've ever seen Vince's hair, you know that's outrageous.

SHAWN: That's the thing. Vince no longer has that hair, but the big pompadour is forever etched in people's minds. I believe his hair is trademarked.

HUNTER: It is. If you look right above where his sideburns are, you will see the little ® right there.

DX

Shane

PARTY POOPERS!

HUNTER: The very same night that we did our Vince and Shane imitation we also dumped three hundred pounds of poop on them. A pretty good night all in all, I'd have to say. But it wasn't that easy to pull off. There is a lot of thought that goes into something like that. Shawn and I had to eat a lot and take a heavy dose of laxatives.

SHAWN: Fortunately, we also had people who could help us out. After all, it's not like Hunter and I could generate all that poop, encase it in some kind of booby trap, and install the trap in the arena. This is where we've been very fortunate. We don't have to put a lot of the practical things in order, we just worry about the big ideas; it's somebody else who has to make it work. I do feel for the guy who had to go to the manure store and say, "I need three hundred pounds of manure." I remember them really having to water it down, because as you know, manure is very dry.

HUNTER: Excuse me, but I don't know if Shawn is even aware of this, but how they actually got all that poop was that they

One of our more inspired ideas.

followed Big Show around for three days. Now, Big Show doesn't drink a lot of liquids, and he eats a lot of bulk, so let's just say it was fairly loggish and we had to water it down so it would have a nice even spread.

SHAWN: Wow! I didn't know that. He looked like he had lost a few pounds that night. Obviously there was a lot of union and hazmat stuff hurdles we had to clear. But we got it all done. I guess you could say DX really stunk up the joint that night!

DX

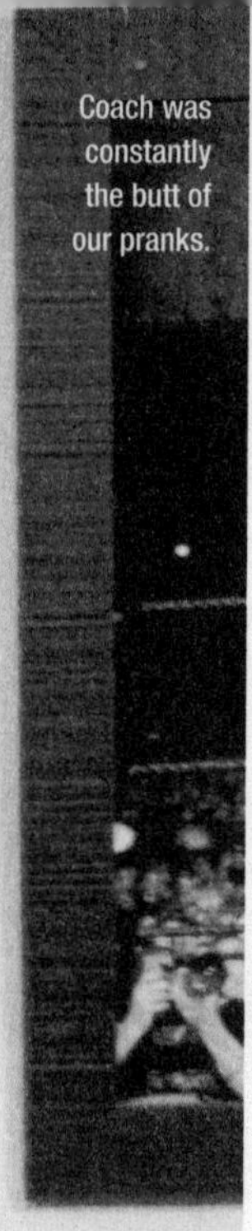
Coach was constantly the butt of our pranks.

BATTLE OF WITS

HUNTER: Vince is a very smart man, but he's in a whole different league when it comes to matching wits with DX. We're good at pushing his buttons and we enjoy it very much. Like the time he banned us from *Raw,* and we still not only got on the show but had this great Fourth of July barbecue in the parking lot, and commandeered the WWE production truck.

SHAWN: Don't forget to mention we set off that green-gas bomb in his limo that night too.

HUNTER: And we set off a green-gas bomb in his limo too. Then the next week he tried to trap us in that three-dollar net he picked up at Toys "R" Us or somewhere like that.

SHAWN: Again, that's the difference between DX humor and Vince McMahon humor. We were getting very Road Runner and Wile E. Coyote. He's symbolic of a lot of people and we're symbolic of a lot of people—we're mainly symbolic of people in the trailer park. He's the uppity-type person who needs to be sophisticated. Poop on people is fun for us, not so much for him. He was very much Wile E. Coyote at this point and making a big mistake trying to keep up with us.

HUNTER: Not to mention it's pretty easy to stay one step ahead of him. On the day of the net drop, all we had to do was read the script earlier in the day, and we clearly saw it say they were going to drop a net on us. That's why I tell all the young Superstars in the locker room how important it is to read the script before the show. They could save themselves a lot of trouble if they would only listen. I guess we could have let it fall on us. After all, it wasn't like a tiger trap. All we would have had to do is pull it off. We pull it off, wait for them to come up, and then give them an ass kicking.

SHAWN: Vince using Coach as his point person to keep us down wasn't the brightest move either. I mean, nothing Coach did to DX ever worked. The fact that he was incompetent from the get-go was gold for us. Coach had already achieved a level of incompetence unmatched in WWE history, and he wasn't afraid to build on his legacy.

HUNTER: He was a great foil for us. He didn't mind doing dumb stuff. To his credit, he doesn't mind getting egg on his face. He has a similar sense of humor; the dumber it is, the more he likes it. I think Coach was the perfect idiot to throw at us. Vince couldn't have lobbed a bigger softball at us.

DX

PARTY TIME

SHAWN MICHAELS

"Boys and girls, the last couple of weeks have been tough for DX and me personally. Other than getting the opportunity to witness a few prison inmates and work on my prison ministry, last week was pretty undesirable. That notwithstanding, as I was sitting there thinking, I began to think to myself, you know, Vince and Shane McMahon have forgotten one very important thing about D-Generation X. You see, there's always been two things that have separated us from absolutely everybody else in this industry. One, we have always done what we want, literally, whenever we want, literally. Like for instance, we have a tendency to focus on Vince McMahon's seemingly voracious . . . for, well, you know . . ."

HUNTER

"But the second thing . . ."

(Here comes the money, here we go money, uh)

JIM ROSS

"The wickedly wealthy have joined us."

SHANE MCMAHON

"You guys are known for a few things. One is, yes, you are known for sophomoric pranks. And the other thing you are known for is, let's see, over the last several weeks you have been known for getting systematically taken out by none other than the chairman of the board, Vincent Kennedy McMahon, and yours truly, Shane O Mac."

VINCE MCMAHON

"There's no doubt that *SummerSlam* is the biggest party of the summer and there's no doubt after *SummerSlam* that we are going to be partying down. But for you two I regret to inform you that your party is over."

HUNTER: *SummerSlam* didn't turn out to be such a party for the McMahons, did it?

SHAWN: No, it didn't. I think you summed it up pretty well the next night on *Raw.*

HUNTER: You mean when I addressed the *Raw* audience from an "undisclosed" location and said, "Ladies and gentlemen, I'm Triple H of D-Generation X. You are probably wondering where I am tonight. It's a long story, but let me give you the quick version. You see, last night, after overcoming Vince and Shane McMahon's master plan to destroy DX—which included but was not limited to the use of cheerleaders, a leprechaun, a limey, a chubby giant, and a cannibal—after overcoming all of that and defeating Vince McMahon at *SummerSlam,* the biggest party of the summer, we were then on our way to Bridgeport and we could not help but notice Vince McMahon's private plane flying overhead . . . Anyway, we came here to this private air terminal where Vince parks his thirty-million-dollar private plane and we just had to see it for ourselves. Unfortunately, a little bit of an incident took place and, well, you should probably see it for yourself."

SHAWN: Wow, that's exactly what you said! How'd you do that?

HUNTER: TiVo, Shawn, TiVo. Remember, Shawn, unlike most other guys in the locker room, I watch the shows.

We do have to say that, for all his bad qualities, Vince knows how to travel in style. We certainly enjoyed taking advantage of his hospitality.

SHAWN: We should probably tell the readers how fun it was to spray-paint Vince's private jet.

HUNTER: It was fun. I mean, the food on the plane was great (thanks, Vince), the stewardesses were hot (thanks, Vince), and just knowing how Vince was going to react, anticipating the look on his face when he saw what we had done, was maybe the best part of all.

SHAWN: I thought his head was going to explode when he saw what we did. You remember what he said?

HUNTER: You mean after he had calmed down a bit, thought he had us, and said, "I suppose you people enjoyed what DX did to my plane. That's a thirty-million-dollar aircraft and you people encourage that kind of degeneracy! Well, I'll tell you who sucks, and it's DX, because in just a few minutes we are going to have *our* fun. See, I've called the cops, and as you all know the airport is right up the street. So we are going to stand right here and watch DX get arrested."

SHAWN: As I recall, we didn't get arrested, did we?

HUNTER: No, we didn't. I believe we left our mark on WWE corporate headquarters.

SHAWN: The old man really lost his mind after that.

HUNTER: That was great, wasn't it?

SHAWN: Of course. For me, the most fun part about agitating Vince is the reaction you get from him. He genuinely gets so upset it's hilarious.

HUNTER: You know he is trying to be calm and not explode, but he can't help himself. When we sent him the penis pump, he didn't think that was funny. Why on earth would you send me a penis pump? No, it *is* funny, and the way you are selling it makes it even more funny. It's almost unintentional on his part.

SHAWN: If he could just ignore our antics and not sell our stuff, we'd be left standing there like two idiots who tried to make a joke and completely bombed.

HUNTER: That's never happened . . . Not possible with Vince. He just can't help himself.

THE VORTEX OF DOOM

SHAWN: This is a moment in our story where we need to be completely serious for a few moments. On September 17, 2006, WWE fans were subjected to one of the most disturbing, repulsive, and horrifying incidents in not just WWE history, but the history of the entire world.

HUNTER: It was ugly, and it was big.

SHAWN: It was us, D-Generation X, sticking Mr. McMahon's head up Big Show's butt. The very same butt that I now know was capable of producing three hundred pounds of poop in just three days.

HUNTER: It's a picture I'll never be able to get out of my head: Five hundred and thirty pounds of glory, covered in blood, and Mr. McMahon . . . Oh, it looked like Shamu giving birth to Vince McMahon. I was actually a little worried for Shawn when this was going on because he's a bit lighter than me. I was worried that he might get sucked into the vortex of Big Show's butt and disappear and never come out again. I don't know if you could see, but I had a rope that I tied around his ankle, and I secured it to the bottom rope in case he started getting sucked in. If this happened, I'd grab the rope and hopefully be able to keep him out.

SHAWN: This precaution actually has biblical roots. In Old Testament times, they had to do that with the priests before they entered the holy tabernacle. If the high priest hadn't washed himself and symbolically cleansed himself of all his sins before entering the holy tabernacle, you never knew what the Lord was going to do. So they used to have to keep a rope tied to the high priest that actually had bells on it, because you never knew when the Lord was going to go, "Hey, you're not cleansed and you entered the most holy place!" And then, *boom!* Fire comes down out of the sky and that's the end of the high priest. They would use the rope to drag the carcass out.

HUNTER: Wow!

SHAWN: So I am just saying, for what it's worth, Hunter was enacting a very scriptural message there when he tied my ankle. Now obviously, Big Show's backside and the tabernacle are very different. One is the most holy place and the other is maybe the least holy.

HUNTER: I see the comparison, but I'm not sure that God's brand of punishment would involve Big Show's rectum.

SHAWN: Was I worried about the possible repercussions of shoving Vince's head up Big Show's rear? If it were just me, HBK, doing it, maybe. But when Hunter and I are together in DX, I have absolutely no fear of repercussions. I guess because we pushed so much years back and they yelled at us a lot, but nothing really happened, I don't have that fear when I am in DX. People enjoy the antics so much that it seems OK.

HUNTER: It was kind of one of those things that even when we were doing DX in the beginning, I don't ever recall being scared to the point where we were like, "Oh boy, we've really done it this time and we are going to get fired." It was so good and the people liked it so much, and the ratings were so good, that it was one of those things that even though they were mad at us, it was so good they had to run with it.

SHAWN: Even now it's like, when my kids do something wrong, you have to tell them on face value that it's wrong, even if it is funny, like passing gas.

HUNTER: Yes, "pull my finger" is humorous at any age. Back to Vince for a second:

As much as we like to torment him, you really have to give him a lot of credit. We were talking about what we were going to do for this match, and someone wanted to have this really brutal match with all kinds of physicality, and we were like, "We don't think this is what people want to see. What they want to see is us sticking Vince's head up Big Show's butt." And Vince is like, "OK. Why don't we do that?" We're like, "OK."

SHAWN: That's why I don't know if I could have another job or work for another person. Because he's just that much off. He's a crazy old bastard, but I love him.

HUNTER: Yeah, you think Bill Gates is letting someone at Microsoft shove his head up someone's butt?

WHAT GOES AROUND COMES AROUND, OR SOMETHING LIKE THAT

SHAWN: After disposing of Big Show and Mr. McMahon, we turned our attention to Randy Orton and Edge—or, rather, they saw an opportunity in coming after us. They decided to pull a "DX" and impersonate us. I'll have to admit that they were pretty funny, given the circumstances.

HUNTER: They were in a bit of a difficult spot because it's really hard to go out and make fun of someone for something they've already made fun of themselves. If it doesn't bother the guy then it's not that humorous. That's the difficult part about coming after us: What are they going to say that we haven't said about ourselves? Whenever anyone tries to make fun of me, they goof on my big nose, but making fun of the obvious isn't always funny.

SHAWN: Yes, I think mentioning your big nose over and over again ceases to be funny at some point, no matter how big it is. It would have been challenging for us to go out there and do impersonations of Edge and Randy. Shane and Vince are much easier to make fun of. 'Taker too. There's a lot of stuff there to work with. When DX did the Nation, there's a lot of stuff there. With us, we are regular guys and it's harder to do. The next week we could have gone out and cut a ten-minute promo on them, but if you watch our response to them, we spent more time cutting on each other than blistering them.

HUNTER: They did as well as they could have. Anybody doing an impersonation other than DX, it almost looks like they are just doing a copy of DX. To me, the stuff with Edge and Randy got good when it turned serious. Which gave DX the opportunity to show both sides of our ability.

SHAWN: I believe that being able to be taken seriously and being able to do the funny stuff really sets DX apart from the rest of the crowd. There's a real art to being able to do something funny but also be taken seriously. We could be in a match pulling someone's pants down having everyone laughing one minute, and then someone would drill me, and *bam!* It's a wrestling match. Psychology-wise, any veteran would tell you that you don't want to do that much "ha ha" and then try to get serious heat on the guy. It won't work most of the time. DX is able to do that. That's one huge reason why DX stands on its own, because we have the ability to laugh and be taken seriously. Fans can be genuinely worried for me getting beat up and then have Hunter come in and clean house.

HUNTER: Guys look at us now and say, "You all used to joke around as DX, how can you tell us not to joke around?" But they had better be able to be taken seriously when it's time to. We could go from being funny one moment to beating the piss out of someone. Those guys haven't established that.

SHAWN: It's hard to explain, but it's very evident. We get a kick out of being able to do something that nobody else can do. That's what makes us better. We're competitive guys and we like to prove that we are the best. We want to show people that you can't run with us.

SHAWN: During our feud with Edge and Randy, we wrestled in a match at *Cyber Sunday* where Eric Bischoff was the special guest referee. We lost the match but beat up old Eric pretty good. We also were able to humiliate Eric on *Raw* after he told us that we were nothing more than a poor imitation of nWo.

HUNTER: He's got a point. Hogan was going bald first. I hear that from guys like Bischoff, but I've never really heard it from fans. How were we trying to be like

We felt so bad about Eric Bischoff running WCW into the ground that we got him "a little something."

nWo? I don't see the similarity between the stuff that we did and the stuff they did. They were just like big bullies that came in and wanted to take over the company.

SHAWN: We were juvenile and sophomoric and rebels.

HUNTER: And the funny thing is that we had the idea to do something like DX long before Kevin and Scotty went to WCW.

SHAWN: If you want to know the difference between DX and nWo, all you have to do is look at the two big finger pokes. Hogan pokes Kevin with his finger, Kevin drops like a sack of bricks, Hogan wins the title, and it ends up killing their company. When Hunter and I did the same thing with the European title, it ignited our company to new heights. Obviously there is something different going on here.

Then again, the whole nWo ripoff thing is more of a pissing contest between Eric Bischoff and WWE. It's always tough for a guy to be saddled with, "Hey, you ran a company into the ground."

Personally I've always found it's better to be one with that situation. When I had the title, ratings didn't do well. It's just one of those things. I could make all the excuses in the world, but the bottom line is, ratings went down, and I get the blame for that and that's how the cookie crumbles.

He had a big multimillion-dollar company and he ran it into the ground. So if he says we were a cheap ripoff of nWo and that helps him sleep at night, God bless him. As much as I don't like to be vengeful, he's the one guy—because he takes himself so seriously and has such an ego—that I didn't mind seeing being made fun of. I know it ate him alive to have to have the role he had here in WWE. He sees himself as the smartest guy in the world, the most sophisticated man to ever be in wrestling, and he blessed all of us with his presence, and we were just fortunate to have been able to breathe the same air as him.

HUNTER: He was a good sport when he came here, but somewhere deep down inside him when Vince had him coming in here, he had to be thinking to himself, "I have to come work for this guy who I said was a big dick, and who I wanted to put out of business. Now I have to eat crap and go work for that guy?" It must have eaten him up inside, and we got to look at him and go "ha ha" every day. There's a little poetic justice there.

SHAWN: You have to remember, when he was the top dog, he wasn't afraid to tell

If Eric Bischoff had met Big Dick Johnson during his WCW days, Bischoff would have probably made Dick a WCW Champion.

everyone how great he was and how much better he was than everyone. He got his in the end. That's justice. When we did the stuff with Big Dick Johnson, he did everything he could to take it like a man, and to his credit he did, but inside you know it just tore him to shreds.

HUNTER: Back a few years, when Bischoff was going to get bronco busted by Mae Young, everyone thought it was going to be hilarious in itself. I had another idea though. I went to Stephanie and said, "We have to talk to Mae because it would be really funny if she put sardines in her underwear." Of course, Mae was all into it and emptied a jar of sardines in her underpants and put her tights on over that. Eric had no idea, and he was never smartened up to it. He thought all that was Mae, and he just suffered.

DX

Rick Flair, honorary member of DX for life.

THE DX PROCLAMATION ON WHO'S IN AND WHO'S OUT

Through the years, there have been a lot of Superstars who claim to be official members of DX. As the founding fathers, and only current members, we—Shawn and Hunter, Hunter and Shawn—would like to set the record straight and clear up one large misunderstanding. We do hereby declare that Hornswoggle, the Great Khali, and Boogeyman were never members of DX.

For a minute or two in 2007, it might have seemed that we let those three into our exclusive club. Many even congratulated us on our benevolence, our willingness to let the less fortunate, the not so popular, join DX and feel like winners.

The fact is that this was about DX trying to get through a promo when the creative team had no idea what to do. That's why we did what we did with Hornswoggle, Boogeyman, and the Great Khali. While we let them hang with us for five minutes until we could get out of there, they never were, are not, and have never been part of DX. There was no benevolence on our part.

At the present time there are only two members of DX. We would, however, like to announce that because of all the admiration we have for Ric Flair, we are inducting him as our first honorary DX member for life. And even if Ric doesn't think this is cool, well, too bad. We want him in and that's that. With this honorary membership, Ric gets an all-axxess pass to anything DX.

As you remember, Ric was with us for a brief time after *Survivor Series* in 2006. He enjoyed it, we enjoyed it, and any time he wants to come back, DX will welcome him back. What you may not know is that Ric wanted to do something with DX where he would have quasi-membership in an offshoot called AARPDX. We're not sure where we are going with this, but it sounds funny so we just thought we'd bring it up.

Anyhow, sometimes when we were at live events and one of the two of us wasn't at the show, the one of us who was there would cut a promo on the one who wasn't there—try saying that five times fast. Invariably, Ric would come out with a DX shirt and just pretend to be the one who wasn't at the show. He'd screw up all our lines and do everything at the wrong time. It was total chaos, and it was beautiful. So Ric, here's to you! You'll always be a DX member to us because you are our inspiration.

SHAWN: If we emulated anyone it would have to be, from a working standpoint, Ric Flair, Dusty Rhodes, and the Four Horsemen. It would take all Four Horsemen to get Dusty down, and then when Dusty made his comeback they would be flying all over the place.

HUNTER: We used that philosophy and style. Everything we did played to the idea that it takes two of us or more to get you down. Sometimes we'd be getting beat up, and Chyna would come in and stop them and then we'd beat them up, and it was like the broad was making the save. It made us that much more despised.

DX
RULZ

D-Generation X, the next generation.

THE END . . . AGAIN . . . FOR NOW

HUNTER: By the time 2007 rolled around, we had had a pretty good run with DX and were in the middle of a good but serious program with Randy Orton and Edge. At *New Year's Revolution*, I gave Randy Orton a spinebuster. When I landed on my knee, my quad just blew up. I managed to finish the match, but it was hurt really bad. I was going to be out for a while, so this run of DX was pretty much over.

SHAWN: I think we were going to go one more match with Randy and Edge. We were starting to wind down DX on the way to *WrestleMania* because they didn't want both of us in one match. DX was so hot at that point that I kept coming out to the DX theme, but there was no thought of bringing someone in to replace Hunter.

HUNTER: I think at this point for either one, if he were to get hurt or I would, it wouldn't be DX without the both of us.

SHAWN: It would be like KISS with the other guitarist who replaced Ace Frehley. It just wouldn't be the same.

HUNTER: It's not like we didn't have success with other guys, and I think the other guys will probably all get mad about what I'm going to say, but to me, DX was always Shawn and I. Now, we did have success with Billy, Road Dogg, and Kid, but it wasn't quite the same. To put anyone else in—with the exception of Flair, of course—I don't think people would accept it. So for better or worse, the world is stuck with Shawn and me forever.

DX

DX
D-GENERATION
HBK
Heart Break
DX
HHH
KING OF KINGS

REFLECTIONS ON ACT III

SHAWN'S MOM

"Can't Hunter be stupid just one time? Why do you always have to play the idiot?"

SHAWN

"Well, I'm a better idiot than he is."

HUNTER: I was a bit surprised at how well DX did when we reunited. It's funny too, because when we went out in the beginning we would say to each other, "Can you believe how over this is?" I think it's a great testament to our fans. We kept waiting for them to boo us and it never happened, and the dumber the stuff we did, the bigger it got.

SHAWN: Since I came back in 2002, talk of a DX reunion had almost been like a quarterly tax return because they asked us about a DX reunion so regularly. But Hunter and I, for the most part, aren't into sequels. Hunter and I didn't want to go back and do a rehash of something we did before, that was a real concern. We weren't sure it would work. This time I got the feeling it would be different.

HUNTER: Also, this time the story line was really building toward it. Shawn was doing the stuff with Vince, and who would naturally come to his aid but his best friend, Hunter.

SHAWN: And once Hunter comes out, you know what that makes it.

HUNTER: And even at that point, they told us it was a one-time thing. We were like, "OK." But as soon as we did it, we couldn't leave it on the table.

SHAWN: I think the term was, we couldn't leave that much money on the table.

HUNTER: At that point in time we saw it was going to be different from before.

SHAWN: Ultimately we are in the people business, and we had to be able to deliver what they wanted. We had to make sure it was good for us creatively. DX has always been about doing things that came natural. Now we aren't as racy as we were before, and the challenge became: How do we bring the same fun to a less edgy DX? Our answer was that in order to do some things that I wasn't so comfortable doing, I had to be so out of touch and dumb.

HUNTER: We did silly stuff with Shawn whenever something racy would happen, like sending him looking for Mr. Fuji when those chicks were going to flash us at the barbecue. Fans knew he was a different person than he was back in '97. For us to pretend that Shawn wasn't different would have been insulting to the fans. Rather than WCW or girls getting boob jobs, this was the eight-hundred-pound gorilla now. We couldn't ignore it. So to get around Shawn's change, we just made him more of an idiot.

SHAWN: I think "more naïve" would be a gentler term.

HUNTER: Sometimes we did stuff that wasn't that funny, but the fact that he was offended by it made it funny.

SHAWN: It's the same with the other eight-hundred-pound gorilla: you know, Hunter's marital situation.

HUNTER: At the time, it was one of those behind-the-scenes topics we didn't want

Shawn has grown and matured. Luckily, Hunter could still deliver the quality juvenile humor.

to hit because it could be a money story line later. (We used it in the lead-up to *WrestleMania 25*.) But some people already knew. So we played around with it.

SHAWN: If you knew you knew and you got the skinny, great, but you don't have to show them pulling the rabbit out of the hat. But we did give them a peek behind the curtain.

THE FUTURE

SHAWN: D-Generation X is WWE's version of the bullpen.

HUNTER: In case of emergency, bring out DX. If the creative team needs something at a Pay-Per-View and there is nothing going, you can be sure the little red phone in our office will go off. The call will be made to DX.

SHAWN: For every person who says I've seen that, that's been done, we believe there's a new generation to corrupt. We corrupted a whole generation of fans, and we'll have future generations to corrupt again . . . there's always going to be that next generation. Just think, right now there are kids who were too young to appreciate what we did in 2006. They will someday be parents and want to show their kids DX, so we owe it to them to continue on someday. We are kind of like a link for generations to connect.

If not for DX, who would have been able to come up with the term *dysfunctional family*? That's a whole new term that was created because guys like us make it possible for families to be dysfunctional.

HUNTER: We like to keep families together on multiple levels. We are a benefit to society. All the other stuff we did, you have to explain to your kid why that's not right to do. We are a teaching tool for families.

SHAWN: And we get them in touch with the hypocrisy of the real world. Parents have to sit there while laughing. When your child laughs, that's when you have to tell them not to. That's when you start to talk and the communication door flies open. Additionally, it supports the famous "Do as I say, not as I do" mantra that all parents quote.

DX

THE SECRET OF OUR SUCCESS

TRIPLE H

"Vince, we know you are angry, your concern is valid. After all, last night you tossed Big Show's salad. We beat you up, you almost kicked the bucket. And if you're not down with that, we got two words for you: Suck it!"

HUNTER: It's hard to believe we've come to the end of our story . . . for now. It's come to the end, so I've taken the liberty to explain it to you if you don't mind.

SHAWN: Going back all the way to the beginning, through all the anger and obnoxiousness, there's always been a subtle sophistication to us. Sometimes it gets lost, like when you drop three hundred pounds of poop on people's heads, but taking a broader view, there is always a little bit of sophistication with us. You see this day in and day out in our work. Every night for I don't know how many years, Hunter's had to come up with something in the introduction.

HUNTER: Every night I try to come up with a different joke or a different line for every city we are in. Sometimes I have nothing, and I've even done that one before: "Folks, I've got nothing, sorry." But I think that one of the things that's funny about DX is the different layers of humor. We can drop poop on you and then do a funny poem or parody someone. And much to Shawn's chagrin, we can do an R-rated show as well as a G-rated show and they are just as funny. We can do family humor and adult humor. If we were a one-trick pony, we wouldn't have lasted.

SHAWN: What I like about this second time—third time for Hunter—is that we made fun of the obvious. We are both older, we are both husbands, we are both fathers, and the thing is, we are part of a generation of parents who haven't forgotten how we were back in high school.

HUNTER: We can try to sound like we are different parents. But it's tough for us to say to our kids, "Don't do dumb stuff. I know I did, but you don't do it."

SHAWN: But I like the fact that we didn't come across like we were still twenty-five and hip about everything.

HUNTER: As you said, we made fun of ourselves and the obvious. I made fun of him losing his hair, which is pretty obvious and, if I may say so, a growing concern—well, maybe that's the wrong term to use.

SHAWN: And I made fun of his Mt. Everest–sized nose, but that gets back to calling out the obvious and being out of touch with what's cool. We always have been able to poke fun at ourselves, and it's smarter for us to do it than have someone else do it.

HUNTER: I think we both have open minds as to what's entertaining and funny, and we can both sit back outside of ourselves and look at ourselves and think about what I would say if I saw this. A part of me is looking at the crowd and I'm thinking that I'm doing this stupid stuff but they are loving it, so that is where I am going to go.

SHAWN: We also try to not take ourselves too seriously. Always in our careers, and despite popular opinion, that's one thing we've always tried not to do. We've known each other long enough that we can kid ourselves and say stuff that others won't say. Like he comes up to me after not seeing me for a while and says, "Holy cow, Hulkster, what's going on?" I know, shut up.

HUNTER: We're secure enough to go there, and if it's funny we can go there. Part of the difference, too, is that the business is different today. Nobody else back then wanted this stuff, and it had to come from an anger position. Now you can make fun of someone and they know it's good—they might be self-conscious about it but know it's good TV and so they let it go.

Back then if we said something about someone that bothered them, they would say, "You can't say that about me."

SHAWN: Back then everyone was trying to keep the eight-hundred-pound gorilla unrecognizable. Today everyone acknowledges it and accepts the gorilla.

HUNTER: I think part of it is that we exposed the gorilla. We were the first ones to point out the gorilla, and everyone acknowledges it.

SHAWN: Back then we pointed out the gorilla and nobody liked that.

HUNTER: And because of that, people got mad and then we got mad at them. Today no one gets mad at the gorilla. Why are we talking about gorillas?

SHAWN: Because we're just being ourselves. That's really the key to everything we've done. It never looks like we are trying to be anything but ourselves. That's why I think we are accepted. That's what my wife tells me.

HUNTER: So be yourself, have fun with your friends, and listen to your wife, or girlfriend, or boyfriend, or mom and dad, but most of all, listen to DX.

How dare anyone call us degenerates!

DX TRIVIA

1. Who are the two most handsome Superstars in WWE history?
   A. Kamala and Eric Bischoff
   B. Bastion Booger and George "The Animal" Steele
   C. Shawn Michaels and Triple H

2. True or False: Linda McMahon was once a member of DX.

3. Who inspired the D-Generation X name by referring to the gang as a bunch of "degenerates"?
   A. Vince McMahon
   B. Jim Ross
   C. Bret "Hit Man" Hart

4. In 2007, ____________ tore his ____________ muscle, leading to the end of D-Generation X (for now) as a full-time group.

5. Which member introduced the crotch chop to DX?
A. Shawn Michaels
B. X-Pac
C. Road Dogg

6. True or False: Both Shawn Michaels and Triple H joined the Vince McMahon Kiss My Ass Club.

7. DX's famous "Let's get ready to SUCK IT!," first spoken by __________, was inspired by famous ring announcer __________.

8. True or False: DX has laid claim to the WWE, Intercontinental, World Tag Team, European, Hardcore, and Women's titles.

9. What is the actual name of the DX Band that performs DX's original entrance theme?
A. The Chris Warren Band
B. Ruthless Aggression
C. Green and Black Attack

10. Which mainstream celebrity was briefly a member of DX?
A. Paris Hilton
B. Mike Tyson
C. Boogeyman

11. In the main event of the *In Your House: D-Generation X* Pay-Per-View, Shawn Michaels defended the WWE Championship against __________.
A. Mankind
B. Goldust
C. Ken Shamrock

12. When they reunited in 2006, Triple H and Shawn Michaels were fond of talking about __________ and his love of ________.

13. True or False: Rated RKO was the only tag team to defeat Shawn Michaels & Triple H in a Tag Team match in the past eight years.

14. DX briefly reunited to take on the Radicalz at *Survivor Series 2000.* Who was the only non–DX member on the team?

A. K-Kwik

B. Kane

C. Stone Cold Steve Austin

15. DX gave then–WWE Commissioner Sgt. Slaughter the nickname ________.

16. True or False: X-Pac is the only Superstar to be a member of both DX and nWo.

17. The New Age Outlaws and X-Pac joined DX after which *WrestleMania*?

A. *WrestleMania XIV*

B. *WrestleMania XV*

C. *WrestleMania 2000*

After HBK left in 1998, D-Generation X kept on rolling with its handsome, intelligent, and incredibly well-endowed new leader.

18. Which hip-hop group contributed a new theme song briefly used by DX?

A. Cypress Hill

B. Three 6 Mafia

C. Run-D.M.C.

19. DX's first official DVD set came out in 2007 and was called __________.

20. In which arena did Shawn Michaels defeat Bret Hart to win the WWE Championship in the infamous "screwjob"?

A. The Molson Centre

B. The Pyramid

C. FleetCenter

21. __________ became the new leader of DX in 1998, when HBK had to retire due to a chronic _____ injury.

22. At which 2007 Pay-Per-View event did DX's full-time partnership come to an end, as of this writing?

A. *WrestleMania*

B. *New Year's Revolution*

C. *Armageddon*

23. True or False: Triple H battled Sgt. Slaughter in a Boot Camp match at *In Your House.*

24. Once _________ left DX in mid-1999, the only two members left were Road Dogg and _________.

25. What noxious substance did Triple H and Shawn Michaels dump on an unsuspecting Vince McMahon, Shane McMahon, and Spirit Squad?

A. Sewage

B. Puke

C. Big Show's feces

26. True or False: Shawn O Mac is a better dancer than Shane O Mac.

27. What happened when Test ran to the ring to attack DX on the 11/11/99 episode of *SmackDown*?
   A. His pants fell down
   B. He broke his nose on the bottom rope
   C. They shaved his head

28. True or False: In 2000, Mae Young announced that she was pregnant with Road Dogg's baby.

29. What was Shane McMahon's derogatory nickname for X-Pac?

30. Who was not a member of The Kliq?
   A. Chyna
   B. X-Pac
   C. Scott Hall

31. True or False: DX convinced Kane to speak his first words on WWE TV.

32. At which *WrestleMania* did the DX band perform the National Anthem?
   A. *WrestleMania 13*
   B. *WrestleMania XIV*
   C. *WrestleMania XV*

33. True or False: Undertaker & Steve Austin were the first opponents of Triple H & Shawn Michaels in their first match as allies back in August 1997.

34. Which former WWE Champion did Shawn Michaels taunt by bringing out a midget version of him on *Raw* the night after beating him in his final WWE match?
   A. Hulk Hogan
   B. Bret "Hit Man" Hart
   C. Randy "Macho Man" Savage

35. Which member of DX portrayed "B'Lo" in the group's infamous parody of The Nation?

A. X-Pac
B. Billy Gunn
C. Road Dogg

36. True or False: In a parody of DX's New Age Outlaws, WCW created a faction called the Old Age Outlaws.

37. Which member of DX would frequently come to the ring chugging a popular energy drink?

A. Triple H
B. Billy Gunn
C. X-Pac

38. Which *WrestleMania* was subtitled *DX-Raided*?

39. What kind of match did DX leader Triple H have with The Rock at *SummerSlam 1998*?

A. Ladder match
B. Steel Cage match
C. Best Two-Out-of-Three-Falls match

40. Which tag team did the New Age Outlaws defeat for the World Tag Team title the same night they joined DX in March 1998?

A. The Headbangers
B. The Godwinns
C. Cactus Jack & Chainsaw Charlie

41. Fighting for the rights to the D-Generation X name, former members X-Pac & ____________ collided with Billy Gunn & ____________ at *Fully Loaded 1999*.

42. True or False: The Mean Street Posse were once members of DX for about ten minutes.

43. Complete these lyrics from the DX theme song: "You better get used to the way the ball ________/I've seen what you got—it ________ in ________."

44. Which DX member had the privilege of throwing his or her own urine on Vince and Shane McMahon?
   A. Shawn Michaels
   B. Triple H
   C. Chyna

45. True or False: Triple H and Shawn Michaels used to pal around with the Conquistadors.

46. The night he returned to WWE and joined DX, X-Pac said: "________, I got some advice for ya. You better not step short, or ________ will go so far up your ____ he'll know what you had for breakfast!"

47. Which group did Vince McMahon use in the battle against the reunited DX in 2006?
   A. The Spirit Squad
   B. Lance Cade & Trevor Murdoch
   C. Morrison & Miz

48. True or False: Both Triple H and Shawn Michaels are among the top ten longest-reigning WWE World Champions in WWE history.

49. At which Pay-Per-View event did Chyna turn against DX?
   A. *WrestleMania XV*
   B. *Royal Rumble 1999*
   C. *SummerSlam 2000*

50. True or False: WWE produced a DX yarmulke.

Answers on page 245.

DX getting ready to give our fans a big holiday treat.

KEY DATES IN D-GENERATION X HISTORY

July 22, 1965	Shawn Michaels is born.
July 27, 1969	Triple H is born.
June 3, 1987	Shawn makes his World Wrestling Federation debut in a Tag Team match with Marty Jannetty against Jimmy Jack Funk & Jose Estrada.
June 10, 1987	Shawn gets fired by Vince McMahon.
July 7, 1988	Shawn comes back to World Wrestling Federation. He and Marty Jannetty wrestle Jose Estrada & Jose Luis Riverá.
April 25, 1995	Triple H makes his World Wrestling Federation debut against Buck Zumhoff.
April 26, 1995	Triple H is welcomed into The Kliq.
July 6, 1995	The Kliq meets with Vince McMahon and suggests that the company needs to take an edgier approach.

May 19, 1996	Shawn, Hunter, Kevin Nash, and Scott Hall break kayfabe in the famous Curtain Call incident at Madison Square Garden.
June 9, 1997	Shawn and Hunter discuss forming a tag team and bringing out Hunter's humorous side aboard the *Wrestle Vessel* in the Gulf of Mexico.
August 18, 1997	Shawn, Hunter, and Chyna make their first appearance together when Shawn wrestles Undertaker in Atlantic City.
September 20, 1997	Shawn and Hunter cause their first riot when they screw Davey Boy Smith out of the European Championship in Birmingham, England.
September 29, 1997	Hunter tells off Vince McMahon for burying him after the Curtain Call, thereby exposing Vince as the owner of World Wrestling Federation.
October 5, 1997	Shawn beats Undertaker in the first ever Hell in a Cell match at *Badd Blood.*
October 6, 1997	Bret Hart calls Shawn and Hunter degenerates. Shawn agrees and christens himself, Hunter, and Chyna as D-Generation X.
November 7, 1997	The Montreal Screwjob.
November 24, 1997	Shawn and Hunter mock Bret about Montreal by reenacting the match with "Midget Bret."
December 8, 1997	The first and only DX Pay-Per-View takes place in Springfield, Massachusetts.
December 9, 1997	D-Generation X plays strip poker in the ring.
December 14, 1997	Shawn and Hunter cause a riot at the Pyramid in Memphis, Tennessee.
December 15, 1997	DX is given a police escort out of Little Rock, Arkansas, after causing another riot. They are told to never come back to the city.
December 22, 1997	Shawn drops the European Championship to Hunter in one of the greatest matches in WWE history.

It is *never* a good idea for friends to get into a sausage-measuring contest.

January 19, 1998	DX performs the "Suck the Cook" sketch when they have a barbecue on *Raw*.
March 3, 1998	Mike Tyson joins DX after hinting that he was going to go after Shawn Michaels.
March 28, 1998	DX and Tyson humiliate Stone Cold Steve Austin in front of 30,000 screaming fans during a special DX workout before *WrestleMania XIV*.
March 29, 1998	Stone Cold Steve Austin beats Shawn for the World Wrestling Federation Championship at *WrestleMania XIV* as Mike Tyson turns on DX.
March 30, 1998	Hunter takes over DX. He brings in X-Pac and welcomes the New Age Outlaws to the group. Shawn goes home to Texas.
April 6, 1998	DX pees on DOA's motorycles, causing thousands of dollars in damage.

Celebrating winning the WWE Championship, DX-style.

April 27, 1998	DX invades WCW in Norfolk, Virginia.
May 12, 1998	DX invades WCW headquarters and the CNN center in Atlanta, Georgia.
July 6, 1998	DX parodies The Nation. The Crock, Mizark, and B'Lo steal the show.
August 30, 1998	Hunter beats The Rock in a Ladder match at *SummerSlam* to win his first Intercontinental Championship.
October 9, 1998	Because of a knee injury, Hunter is stripped of his title for not defending it within thirty days.
November 23, 1998	Shawn returns to WWE for a brief stint as commissioner. Chyna settles a sexual harassment suit (in a story line) with Mark Henry and DX parodies the Corporation.
January 4, 1999	Shawn rejoins DX for one night but gets beaten up by the Corporation and leaves to go home to Texas and have back surgery. DX celebrates with Mankind when he wins the Championship from The Rock.
January 25, 1999	Chyna gives Hunter a low blow and leaves DX to join the Corporation.
March 8, 1999	On *Raw,* Chyna holds Hunter so that Kane can shoot a fireball at him, but Hunter ducks and the fireball accidentally burns Chyna's face.
March 28, 1999	At *WrestleMania XV,* Hunter beats Kane when Chyna double crosses Kane and reunites with Hunter. Hunter and Chyna turn on X-Pac during his match with Shane McMahon and they beat up the New Age Outlaws when they come to X-Pac's defense.
March 29, 1999	On *Raw,* Hunter and Chyna cease to be part of DX, which is now led by X-Pac.
August 23, 1999	Hunter wins his first World Championship by defeating Mankind in Ames, Iowa.
October 25, 1999	DX reunites when X-Pac and Hunter aid the New Age Outlaws in their match against Steve Austin & Mankind.

November 15, 1999	Hunter challenges Vince to a match at *Armageddon* after DX lights Vince's office on fire.
November 29, 1999	Hunter shocks the world during the wedding of Stephanie McMahon and Test by showing footage of Stephanie's bachelorette party in Las Vegas the night before. After paying off a bartender to drug Stephanie's drink, Hunter took a knocked-out Stephanie to an all-night wedding chapel and married her. Hunter and Stephanie are married!
December 12, 1999	Hunter beats Vince in a No Holds Barred match at *Armageddon* after nearly breaking his leg earlier in the day. Stephanie turns on Vince and aligns herself with Hunter.
February 15, 2000	The DX Express makes its debut. DX locks Kane and Paul Bearer in the luggage hold and drives off with them in it.
March 28, 2000	DX provides some interference to help Stephanie McMahon-Helmsley win the Women's Championship from Jacquelyn.
April 2, 2000	At *WrestleMania 2000*, Triple H, with a little help from Vince McMahon, retains the WWE Championship.
April 25, 2000	Stone Cold Steve Austin destroys the DX Express.
May 21, 2000	At *Judgment Day*, Triple H defeats Rock in an Iron Man match to win back the World Championship.
November 6, 2000	Hunter re-forms DX for one night only. DX takes on and defeats the Radicalz.
July 22, 2002	Shawn Michaels makes his long-awaited return to WWE. Triple H teases that he wants to re-form DX with Shawn but ends up turning on and Pedigreeing his former friend.
August 25, 2002	At *SummerSlam*, Shawn defeats Triple H in his first match back.
November 17, 2002	At *Survivor Series*, Shawn defeats Triple H in an Elimination Chamber match to win the World Championship.

December 26, 2005	Shane McMahon viciously attacks Shawn Michaels with a chair and forces Shawn to join the Vince McMahon Kiss My Ass Club.
March 6, 2006	Stephanie McMahon drugs Shawn Michaels's water bottle and Shane and Vince subsequently destroy him in two matches on the same night.
April 2, 2006	At *WrestleMania 22,* Shawn Michaels defeats Vince McMahon in a No Holds Barred match.
June 12, 2006	After Triple H avoids joining the Vince McMahon Kiss My Ass Club, Vince sends the Spirit Squad after him. Shawn Michaels makes the save for his old friend.
June 19, 2006	DX officially reunites and spray-paints the letters "DX" on Vince McMahon's executive assistant Jonathan Coachman's butt. They dump green slime on the Spirit Squad and make fun of them by bringing out a team of midget Spirit Squaders. They also send Vince a penis pump, which doesn't sit too well with the WWE Chairman.
June 25, 2006	At *Vengeance,* DX beats the Spirit Squad in a Five-on-Two Handicap match. They celebrate by shoving the face of one Spirit Squad member in Triple H's butt.
June 26, 2006	Triple H and Shawn parody the McMahons. Triple H plays Vince and Shawn plays Shane. The highlight of the impersonation comes when both dance to Vince McMahon's "Stand Back." Later in the show, DX drops three hundred pounds of Big Show's excrement on Vince, Shane, and the Spirit Squad.
July 3, 2006	Vince McMahon bans DX from the building. DX has a barbecue in the parking lot. After partying, DX takes over the WWE production truck and plays havoc with a Vince McMahon promo. When Vince leaves *Raw* in his limousine, a gas bomb goes off and Vince emerges covered in green powder.

Look to WWEShop.com for DX Glow Sticks, as well as all your other D-Generation X merchandise needs!

July 10, 2006	Vince McMahon invites DX to *Raw* in a futile attempt to drop a net on them. Shawn Michaels and Hunter mock Vince for trying to pull such a lame trick.
July 15, 2006	*On Saturday Night's Main Event*, DX destroys the Spirit Squad in a Five-on-Two Elimination match.
July 17, 2006	DX begins a new tradition of blatantly shilling their merchandise on *Raw*.
July 24, 2006	Triple H, Vince, and Stephanie are not at the arena because Stephanie McMahon is giving birth to her second child. Shawn Michaels is forced to wrestle the Spirit Squad by himself and looks to be on his way to victory until Umaga runs in and destroys Shawn.
July 31, 2006	Vince and Shane McMahon gloat about Vince's new granddaughter, and they announce that they will be facing DX in a tag match at *SummerSlam.* DX interrupts their promo and Triple H brags about the guy who "knocked" Stephanie up. The McMahons plant Cuban cigars on Triple H and he is arrested by FBI agents. Shawn loses to Umaga after Vince, Shane, and the Spirit Squad aid the Samoan Bulldozer.
August 7, 2006	Shawn Michaels gets arrested after attacking Shane McMahon in front of a group of policemen. With help from Vince and Shane, Umaga beats Triple H.
August 20, 2006	At *SummerSlam,* DX beats Vince and Shane McMahon.
August 21, 2006	DX "hijacks" Vince McMahon's personal jet and spray-paints "DX" on it. Vince threatens to have the police arrest DX for vandalism. DX then moves to WWE corporate headquarters and spray-paints "DX" all over the building. Vince has an emotional breakdown. Vince and Shane leave the arena in their limousine, only to have DX connect a chain to the rear axle and subsequently destroy the limousine as it tries to leave the arena. Vince has a nervous breakdown.

August 28, 2006	Vince and Shane McMahon enlist the help of Big Show to try and destroy DX.
September 5, 2006	DX wrestles Big Show in a Handicap match, and Hardcore Holly interferes before DX can get the victory.
September 17, 2006	At *Unforgiven*, DX defeats Vince, Shane McMahon, and Big Show in a Handicap Hell in a Cell match. During the match, DX shoves Vince's head up Big Show's butt.
October 16, 2006	Randy Orton and Edge impersonate DX. DX responds by making fun of Edge's and Orton's "manliness."
November 5, 2006	At *Cyber Sunday*, Eric Bischoff is voted the special guest referee for DX's match against Rated RKO. DX beats up Bischoff but loses the match to Edge & Orton. Bischoff manages to recover and count the pinfall.
November 6, 2006	Vince McMahon puts Eric Bischoff in charge of *Raw* for the night. Bischoff bans DX from the building and makes a match between Rated RKO and Ric Flair & Roddy Piper. DX interferes and secures the win for Flair & Piper. To celebrate, they bring out Big Dick Johnson to dance and grind on Eric Bischoff.

Sorry about your car, Vince.

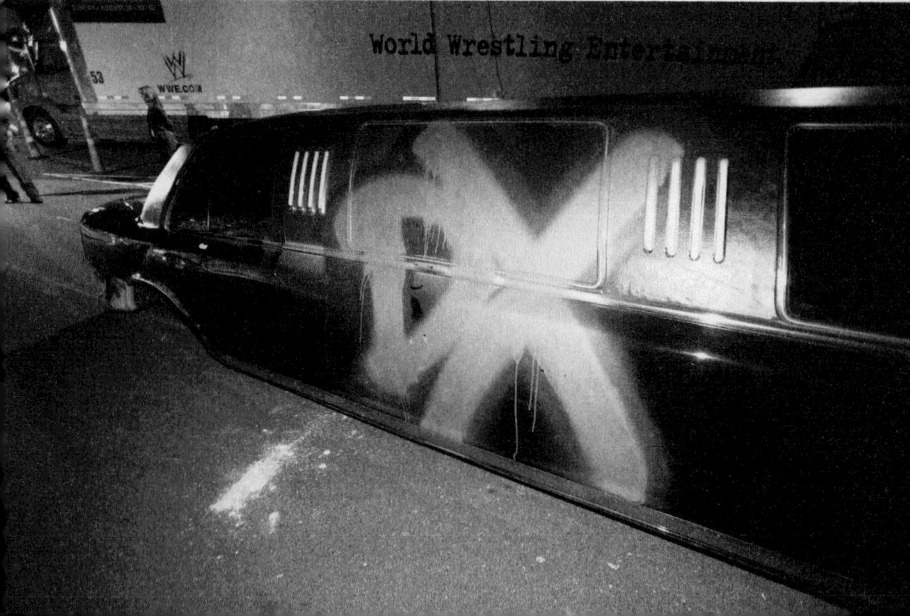

November 13, 2006	Coach offers a $10,000 bounty to any Superstar who can take out DX. Many Superstars take the bait, but DX humiliates them all. In one of their more ingenious acts, they boot themselves from *Raw* and collect the $10,000 for themselves.
November 26, 2006	At *Survivor Series*, the DX team consisting of Triple H, Shawn Michaels, C. M. Punk, and the Hardys shut out Rated RKO: Edge, Randy Orton, Johnny Nitro, Gregory Helms, and Mike Knox.
November 27, 2006	On *Raw*, Ric Flair joins DX for one night. Rated RKO viciously attacks Flair.
January 7, 2007	At *New Year's Revolution* Triple H blows his quad out while DX is wrestling Rated RKO. The match ends in a no contest. Triple H is shelved for several months.
November 5, 2007	Vince orders DX to reunite for one night only and orders them to wrestle Randy Orton & Umaga. Hornswoggle, Boogeyman, and Great Khali attempt to join DX.
January 28, 2008	DX reunites one more time after Triple H picks Shawn Michaels to be his Tag Team partner in a match against Umaga & Gene Snitsky.
September 29, 2008	DX reunites yet again for one night only when Triple H & Shawn Michaels defeat Lance Cade & Chris Jericho in a Tag Team match.
November 3, 2008	DX reunites one more time for one night only to help celebrate *Raw*'s eight hundredth episode. They are still the most over Superstars on the show.

LIVES
SUCK IT
DX
HBK
D X
HHH
DX
DX
SUCK IT
Are You Ready?
DEGENERATION
HE DIED FOR ME
I'LL LIVE FOR HIM
JOHN 3:16
D-GENERATION

DX TRIVIA ANSWERS

1. C
2. False
3. C
4. Triple H, quadriceps
5. B
6. False
7. Triple H, Michael Buffer
8. True
9. A
10. B
11. C
12. Vince McMahon, cocks
13. True
14. A
15. Sgt. Slobber
16. False
17. A
18. C

19. The New and Improved D-Generation X
20. A
21. Triple H, back
22. B
23. True
24. Billy Gunn, X-Pac
25. C
26. True
27. B
28. False
29. X-Punk
30. A
31. True
32. B
33. False
34. B
35. C
36. True
37. C
38. *WrestleMania XIV*
39. A
40. C
41. Road Dogg, Chyna
42. False
43. bounces, measures, ounces
44. A
45. True
46. Hulk Hogan, Eric Bischoff, ass
47. A
48. True
49. B
50. True